Planning for Success

Planning for Success

Strategies that Enhance
the Process of Goal Attainment

Louis J. Pepe

ROWMAN & LITTLEFIELD
Lanham • Boulder • New York • London

Published by Rowman & Littlefield
An imprint of The Rowman & Littlefield Publishing Group, Inc.
4501 Forbes Boulevard, Suite 200, Lanham, Maryland 20706
www.rowman.com

6 Tinworth Street, London SE11 5AL, United Kingdom

British Library Cataloguing in Publication Information Available

Library of Congress Cataloging-in-Publication Data

ISBN 9781475854459 (cloth : alk. paper)
ISBN 9781475854466 (pbk. : alk. paper)
ISBN 9781475854473 (electronic)

∞™ The paper used in this publication meets the minimum requirements of
American National Standard for Information Sciences—Permanence of Paper
for Printed Library Materials, ANSI/NISO Z39.48-1992.

This book is dedicated to my daughter, Jessica, who understood planning from an early age and watched our lives transform from "one day" to reality —she has been a source of inspiration, pride, and ideas, whom I continue to learn from and prosper from her knowledge and enthusiasm for new technologies.

My inspiration is drawn from iconic leaders in history who came from humbling beginnings only to rise up and achieve great feats: Benjamin Franklin, Alexander Hamilton, and Abraham Lincoln and influential authors James Collins, Steven Covey, and Simon Sinek along with contemporaries who continue to impart wisdom, knowledge, and mentorship—special among them, 2019 Association of School Business Officials President and fellow ASBO Eagle Winner (2015) Claire Hertz, Deputy Superintendent of Business & Operations, Portland Public Schools, Portland Oregon.

Contents

Contents

Foreword

The promise that author and successful business professional Louis Pepe gives is simple, adaptive, and most of all effective. If you read, study, and apply the principles and tactics he outlines in *Planning for Success*, we, our teams and organizations, can rapidly, profoundly, and sustainably increase the probability of success in any goal, large or small. In addition, the insight he provides will have a positive impact on the mindset, morale, and commitment of the people we depend on to achieve our goals and objectives.

Planning for Success takes us on a journey toward goal achievement, starting with a practical approach to properly setting goals, how to plan achievement, how to establish personal value and financial benefits of those goals, preparing for the what ifs, and finally the very important succession planning. All of this is artfully put together in one powerhouse of a book. Based on years of proven and profitable experience, Louis reveals to us how to leverage our teams' potential, talents, know-how, energy, and commitment. This easy-to-read, easy-to-follow information will maximize and sustain the results we ultimately want to achieve.

During my time working with people and organizations, I've observed that very talented, well-educated, and experienced leaders and individuals, after working so hard on a set goal, investing time and resources and activities to achieve that goal, fell short. When this happens, it is often because their thinking failed them—not their management or leadership skills but their thinking about a core belief that they failed to put at the center of all of their strategies. If that core belief is not sound and accurate, every subsequent decision can actually have a negative impact on the probability of success of any goal they pursue.

The core belief I am mentioning here is the uncompromised belief that sound, solid, foolproof, and *effective planning* is the foundation and force of any goal worth stretching toward. This force will motivate, inspire, and create certainty and confidence toward achieving any goal, any size, personal and professional. The belief that goals, budget, objectives, strategies, and results are all dependent on the power and energy of a *sound effective plan* is something all of us need to adopt.

> *Give me six hours to chop down a tree,*
> *and I will spend the first four sharpening the ax.*

These words were apparently stated by Abraham Lincoln. Sounds crazy? It's true. Mr. Lincoln knew that the more time spent on *effective planning*, the higher the probability of success. And there is an abundance of evidence throughout history to prove it. Louis shares a few examples in this book.

So what's the point? The more time we spend sharpening our plans, the easier it is to cut through the obstacles (I call "chaos factor") of life that interfere with the probability of success of our goals. The lack of effective planning causes more problems beyond the obvious—not achieving success. Human behavioral research indicates that employees in organizations or on teams suffering from lack of solid planning are more likely to experience lower morale and compromise commitment.

Teams involved in projects that are not supported by plans that were well thought out, sharpened to a razor's edge, can affect engagement levels. Why? Because the team may adopt a mindset of uncertainty and unpredictability and feel it is too hard to control the outcome. This depressing conclusion can only be seen as a serious threat to any project and will negatively impact productivity and success.

As the new, complex economy continues to unfold, one thing is certain. Our need to do more with less is paramount to our personal as well as our organization's success and growth. We must deepen our insight and adopt new ways of getting the job done. All of this is supported by *Planning for Success.* My appreciation for the valuable knowledge and insight revealed in this book started in the very first chapter. Louis's style of writing is easy to follow and enjoyable. He shares his personal and professional experience and what he learned and observed throughout his successful career, deep diving into all aspects of effective planning, planning for success, paragraph by paragraph. I found myself reflecting on past projects I experienced and realized if I had this book and followed its counsel, the results would have been much higher.

Planning for Success is based on two principles. First, comprehensive planning better prepares us for the temporary defeats we will experience when we are pursuing worthwhile goals. Second, sound planning sharpens our vision of the future, which gives us hope. Hope in the future is power in the present. That power cultivates optimism and purpose, which provides the very energy we need to execute to the max on goals and success—the achievement of our goals.

If you are an individual or leader looking to achieve new, exciting, worthwhile goals in life or business—this book will no doubt have a high, positive influence on how to think about and approach your goals. This work by Louis Pepe is a must read for all who desire success. *Enjoy your journey!*

Dennis Bundinich
Chief Culture Officer, Investors Bank
Short Hills, New Jersey

Preface

A pessimist sees the difficulty in every opportunity; an optimist sees the opportunity in every difficulty.

—Winston Churchill

REALITY-BASED LEADERSHIP (RBL)©:
A CONCEPTUAL FRAMEWORK OF COMMON SENSE

The RBL series is written based on my thirty years of management experience in building, managing, and leading teams to achieve desired outcomes while completing tasks, implementing strategies, and accomplishing goals. This is necessary in any organization to accomplish the ultimate objective—the mission.

Each book is meant to provide a glimpse into differing facets of organizational management that allows for continued success through refinement of skills promoting operational awareness in today's rapidly evolving world of business.

Planning is critical to success and goal attainment in any industry, company, organization, or team. Challenges are why we exist as managers and leaders. It is what allows for the value add that each of us possess to showcase talents and employ problem-solving skills in providing solutions that work. Planning is what allows us to meet those challenges and prevail.

The Germans have a saying, *Stirred in the front, does not burn in the back* or better yet . . . be aware of it and take care of it . . . up front. The time to address any complex issue is in the planning phase. Planning is an effective tool to alleviate problems later.

**Vorne gerührt,
brennt hinten nicht an**

"Stirred in the front, does not burn in the back"

Again the phrase is one I have borrowed from my German wife and use at every opportunity to underscore the importance of prior planning to steer clear of complications later. The saying is great to get the point across and even better to put into practice.

This common saying encourages individuals to clarify issues early through proper and effective planning in order to avoid problems on the back end. This is especially true of conflicts. By addressing issues through considerations and actions, we are dealing with those issues head-on rather than allowing negative outcomes or conflicts to smolder. Timely detection of issues early on can prevent major difficulties later that are susceptible to escalation.

The subject matter in this book is not just advice for the reader; it is tried and true evidence of success and failure experienced by many who value the importance of planning and understand the connection to the accomplishment of daily tasks leading to goal attainment.

Over a thirty-plus-year career in leadership, team building, and management, this is something that I have worked to master and continue to seek improvements whenever and wherever possible. That's how important it is, and it starts with understanding the value of planning.

Nobody plans to fail; however, most people fail to plan, or as Benjamin Franklin put it, "If you fail to plan, you are planning to fail!"

I have found the best planners are those who exhibit the ability to analyze, prioritize, communicate, and think critically, strategically, realistically, and globally—but most important they must have the ability to execute and follow up. If you cannot implement the plan, the plan is just a waste of time and effort.

Louis J. Pepe
Lincoln Park, 2020

Acknowledgments

I have to start by thanking the US Army for the training and leadership development that was bestowed on me from basic training in Fort Jackson, South Carolina, to Primary Leadership Development Course Training (PLDC) in Bad Tölz, Germany, to NCO Academy training in Fort Gordon, Georgia. These multifaceted training programs provided me with practical application and leadership skills that I continue to draw from in my current leadership roles.

Vision, strategy, mission, and organization—the US Army represents the best example of investment in personnel to identify, train, and develop future leaders who are adaptive, disciplined, and ready to lead.

All the Way, Echo 9-2-1, Fort Jackson, South Carolina 1982

C. Co. 11th Signal Battalion, 32nd Air Defense Artillery, E.L.K. Darmstadt, Germany, 1982–1984

USAISC Fort Campbell, Kentucky, 101st Air Assault "Screaming Eagles," 1984–1985

534th Signal, 66th MI Brigade, Munich, Germany, 1985–1988

A very special thanks to Joe Gerberaux, Susan Giordano, and Matt Cavanaugh, former managers with the A&P, for recognizing my leadership potential and allowing me to better myself under their leadership.

I'm forever indebted to Pat George for putting me in touch with Tom Koerner at Rowman & Littlefield Publishers, and Jeff McCausland, founder and CEO of Diamond6 Leadership and Strategy, LLC, for guiding me on the book proposal process. It is because of their efforts and encouragement that I have a legacy to pass on to my colleagues and leaders in the many fields of management.

Part I

THE PROCESS OF PLANNING

Chapter One

Goal Setting

The Difference between Strategies and Objectives (How vs. What)

In order to be successful we need goals; without goals, our plans will never take shape or at least will prove ineffective over time. Without goals we are lost and have no direction.

Goals and objectives are similar in purpose and intent; yet they are different, and each has a separate meaning and purpose. Their similarity tends to create confusion in both identification and formulation; however, their interdependency is what allows each to provide success and attainment for the other with *goals*, representing the broader group or set, and *objectives*, representing the smaller part or subset of that group.

Mike Morrison, a recognized change agent and consultant, considers the difference between goals and objectives as a destination versus a measure of progress, "A goal is a description of a destination, and an objective is a measure of the progress that is needed to get to the destination."[1]

Goals are established to move us forward in life both personally and professionally. In organizations, they form the reason for existence and define the expectations of the shareholders, stakeholders, and directors. Much importance has been placed on goal setting to ensure goals are strategic and focused in order to achieve desired results or outcomes. As Steven Covey puts it, "Begin with the end in mind." In other words, know where you want to go.

When we know what we want, we figure out how to get it. Planning is what allows us to go after it in a way that ensures our success in obtaining the item(s) we desire. Without a plan we are just making a grab or taking a stab at getting lucky in acquiring what it is that we try for, *the prize*. The problem is when others are also seeking the same thing(s) we seek and they too are set on achieving or acquiring them. Now, the race is on, and competition means we need to strategize. First, we need to be sure of what it is we wish to achieve—that's where goals come in to play. Goals keep us focused and provide direction. They provide targets to channel our actions, and as the SMART chart points out, they should be *measurable* and *attainable*. Goals that are not attainable are not goals at all; they are a fantastic but vain hope or pipe dream that dampens our spirit and discourages those we lead when we fall short or fail to achieve the goal. Nobody likes failure, and nobody wants to fail. Additionally, it damages our credibility with those we report to and those who look to us to lead.

Figure 1.1.   SMART Criteria

CASE IN POINT: OVERESTIMATING PRODUCTION

In 1989 I worked for a small automatic grease feeder company SL LUBE/ Systems, Inc., in Elmwood Park, New Jersey. The company was a subsidiary of the larger corporation SL Industries, headquartered in Mount Laurel, New

Jersey. During my time at SL LUBE it was plain to see the company was struggling, as the parent company kept requiring more in sales targets yet reducing staff and cutting back on investments in equipment and R&D for new product lines. More troubling was the quarterly goals agreed to by our CEO that were unrealistic and unachievable. Each time she traveled to corporate headquarters to review and plan the next quarterly operations targets, she would return with unrealistic goals linked to production and sales that far exceeded market demand and current sales.

Not only were the goals beyond our reach; they served to demoralize the floor supervisor and production team and signaled the end of growth opportunities for the business. It was a foreshadowing of the end for the company. It was clearly a desperate move by a desperate executive who believed the promise of future gains would keep the parent company at bay and avoid being sold off or closed down.

"By the 1990s SL found itself struggling financially, no longer followed by investment analysts."[2] I left in 1991. The group was sold off shortly afterward. What stayed with me was the negative feeling associated with overpromising and underdelivering with respect to the setting of goals by the CEO/president. As a result I adopted my own motto of "*underpromise—overdeliver.*" It has since been adopted by a successful food service management company, Pomptonian Food Service, Inc., located in Fairfield, New Jersey, serving more than 400 primary and secondary school locations across New Jersey and recently recognized by *Food Management* magazine's Top 50 Contract Management Companies 2019.

This should not be confused with *stretch goals*, as any worthy goal requires work. If we wish to improve and reach higher attainment of performance, we need to continuously raise the bar. Again, it must be attainable, thus realistic. If reached too easily, it is not a real accomplishment and therefore not a *SMART* goal at all.

Specific and *measurable* are also major components of success in goal setting, as they pave the way for understanding and monitoring of progress. Specificity demands focus and avoids ambiguity. It allows for the delivery of messages that are clear, concise, and to the point when addressing employees and or the public of your intentions, desires, and ultimate outlook—where the company is going and what lies ahead. What is expected (outcomes), and what is sought (results)? Larger goals require longer periods of time to reach and checkpoints along the way to ensure progress is being made. As a result we must incorporate measures to verify and validate the progress.

Goals fall into two basic categories: quantitative and qualitative. When formulating goals you need to ensure you provide both types in order to achieve balanced results. Such an offering ensures a holistic approach to management of the organization's desired results. Each focuses on different drivers and outcomes, and each is measured in different ways. While quantitative goals are directly supported by data, qualitative goals are experienced or perceived, felt rather than directly measured.

Let's examine the difference in the two by looking at the health benefits plan and organizational goals relating to employee health. The goals should translate to better claims experience, fewer claims, and/or fewer high-cost claims, reduced absenteeism, and happier, healthier employees.

- Quantitative Goal: Reduce the number of claims by x percent over the next year by implementing two new employee wellness initiatives.
- Qualitative Goal: Improve employee work–life balance to reduce stress and develop employees who are more loyal, attentive, and committed.

In the quantitative goal, one could easily measure the claims performance against the prior periods to see if the data supports measurable progress. Likewise, the goal in this area is easy to measure by virtue of the fact it happened or not and can be measured over time through data contained in monthly and quarterly reports, thus *relevant* and *timely*. The goal is measurable in data such as claims volume, experience rating, and ultimately a lower renewal percentage.

When setting quantitative goals you need to focus on specific results that are measurable and available to you, such as financial, operational, or numerical metrics. A specific set of metrics provides greater guidance and brings more value to the process. Broad metrics and overarching concepts invite vagueness and misinterpretation on the part of your team.

In contrast, the qualitative goals are harder to measure, as they center on feelings, mood, and culture, like customer satisfaction and employee morale. When measuring goal achievement in this category, as with our example above, one would need to look at multiple measures, such as surveys, retention rates, and employee attendance. However, keep in mind the difficulty with retention and attendance is that both can be influenced by other factors, such as departures for higher compensation, better opportunities, or shorter commutes, and increased sick time absences could be for wellness checks and other doctor visits that are for preventive care. What you can do when measuring absenteeism is look at trends pre- and post-implementation of strategies and development of goals related to attendance. By comparing year-over-year or seasonal data, you have the ability to isolate trends while checking for excessive absenteeism within any group, department, or individual. High absenteeism is also linked to employee satisfaction and evidenced in situations of low morale. Although it requires more effort and construct of data, it is available nonetheless and can prove effective in verifying the attainment of this particular qualitative goal.

A better indication of success with these types of goals might require a closer look at overall productivity and whether implementation of the strategies related to the goal(s) has had a positive effect on output, efficiency, and overall quality of work product. In other words—is the job getting done better, and do the employees appear happy in doing it?

Likewise, exit interviews as well as referrals can provide anecdotal information to measure employee satisfaction. When employees are willing to encourage friends and close acquaintances to work in your firm, company, or organization, it is a testimonial of loyalty and respect. It is without question the ultimate endorsement.

Goals and objectives allow us to work toward results we wish to attain and monitor our progress along the way. They provide important checkpoints to ensure we are on track and guard against deviation from what it is we want. In business that usually means higher profit margins, increased market share, and improved financial positions. In education that means higher student success rates, better test scores, and improved career readiness with acceptance into the most prestigious colleges and universities or technical schools throughout the country. All major organizational goals rely on smaller goals within the organization that optimize departmental operations in furtherance of the larger goals. Goals and objectives also help us evaluate our employees, and in turn with personal improvement plans (PIPs), they allow our employees to evaluate themselves.

Goals state our intentions. They should be clear, direct, and focused—*what we want*, *why we need it*, and *how it will benefit us*. When people understand the goal, that's good; when they like the goal, even better; when they want the goal, it is a great goal, and it will receive a great effort as long as everyone or the majority views the goal in the same way or with the same benefit.

Goals are everywhere—they are found in every type of business and every industry. They are found in our personal lives, as we too wish to achieve better results, such as health goals, family goals, financial goals, career goals, and happiness. They give us direction, focus, and purpose the same way as they guide organizations. Objectives become critical milestones in achieving our personal goals as well.

The importance of objectives and goal setting can be found over several websites, as their value is clearly understood by those who are intent on succeeding. RideAmigos,[3] a TDM (transportation demand management) solution company intent on changing the way the world commutes, is just one quick example.

TDM is the flip side of infrastructure. It focuses on understanding how people make their transportation decisions and helping people use the infrastructure in place for transit, ridesharing, walking, biking, and telework. It is cost-effective in guiding the design of our transportation and physical infrastructure so that alternatives to driving are naturally encouraged and our systems are better balanced.[4]

According to their website, Jeffrey Chernick and Evan Meyer, founders of RideAmigos, have been best friends since the third grade. They have a shared system of values and put it into their mission and everything they do at RideAmigos. They believe in the importance of objectives and goal setting, and put it out plainly on their site, calling them really, really, really important: "Objectives and goals are important to a successful TDM program. How important? Really, really, really important. Why are they so important? Without objectives and goals, it's hard to focus your TDM programming enough to accomplish anything."[5]

So as you can see, the goal here, *"To find alternatives to driving that are naturally encouraged and our transportation systems are better balanced,"* requires objectives that RideAmigos will help you achieve through their software tools. As populations in cities increase and infrastructure becomes more challenged to keep up with demand, the goals' importance increases.

In schools we live on goals—they help our students strive to make progress and attain better results. They require generation of objectives that help us with goal attainment, like SGOs (student growth objectives), to focus in on academic success through evidence-based growth or progress.

The US Department of Education has identified four Agency Priority Goals (APGs)[6] for FY 2018–2019, believing that improving education starts with allowing greater decision-making authority at the state and local levels and empowering parents and students with educational options.

As managers, goals are the targets we need to reach. Objectives provide us with the tools to properly outfit our teams on the treks, both long and short. Before we can accomplish them we need to understand them and buy in to them the same way we expect our people to buy in. Once we are there, we can begin to plan.

Chapter Two

How to Plan

Seven Principles of Planning

Planning, like any other worthwhile activity, is a process requiring varying degrees of thought, research, analysis, and action. It begins by recognizing the fact it is primary, preeminent, and most important in achieving any goal or set of goals in any organization.

When it comes to principles of planning there is a plethora of models, diagrams, and thoughts on essential steps and components; however, in reality, effective planning starts with understanding and applying these seven core principles:

1. Goal Recognition
2. Consideration of Objectives
3. Situational Understanding
4. Consideration of Alternatives
5. Action Timelines
6. Flexibility
7. Strategies

Each principle acts as an essential element in the planning process, allowing managers to engage others necessary to the success of any plan. That effectuates buy-in and ensures all stakeholders have the same *focus*, *energy*, and *drive* while working toward common goals that are structured or framed as SMART goals.

Figure 2.1.   Seven Principles of Planning

1. GOAL RECOGNITION

Planning without recognition of the goals is like taking a drive without a destination or even knowing where you are going—you're just driving to drive. The drive then becomes a tireless journey with no end in sight. Eventually, you either have to turn back or run out of gas. If driving in an area that is unfamiliar or out of range, you could even get lost, or worse yet, break down. That is not how we plan, nor an effective way to accomplish any meaningful task(s) or let alone achievement of any goal or set of goals.

Recognition of goals is what gives purpose and meaning to the formulation of objectives that allow us to manage and achieve those goals.

"Setting goals is not about the accomplishment itself. It is also not just about 'becoming the person required to attain those goals.' That's too fluffy.

It is much deeper, and more important. It is about combining the fortitude to achieve with clear thinking, while making sense of your purpose and defining your ability to deliver value to others."[1]

Properly applying goals is all about effective planning, and goals are the starting point for any plan.

2. CONSIDERATION OF OBJECTIVES

When we start with goals we are thinking Big! This means big initiatives and directional outcomes. Where we want to be!

In order to get there through the accomplishment of the goal(s), we must employ and achieve a set of objectives by creating clear definitive steps in the process of goal attainment.

According to Jeff Boss in a January 2017 *Forbes* article, "When you set a goal you naturally direct your attention toward a next step and, as a result, lead yourself in the right direction which forces your actions—your behaviors—to follow."[2]

Objectives are what allow us as managers to operationalize our goals by laying out the strategies to achieve those goals. Without them, we simply flounder and become overwhelmed—biting off more than we can chew or simply feel incapable of accomplishing the goal that now looms large with no clear path to get there.

3. SITUATIONAL UNDERSTANDING

In order to effectively plan, one must have an understanding of the situation that exists beyond mere awareness. You can be aware of something yet not fully understand it. Moving beyond awareness to reach understanding requires effort and research. This requires a deeper dive into the subject matter through available data for analysis. This provides an understanding of the cause-and-effect relationship regarding your expectation, problem, deficiency, or shortfall and an inventory of available resources both human and capital. Once you have a firm grasp of what is at stake, you can begin to develop a plan that will accomplish your objectives and ultimately the attainment of your goal.

"Situational understanding (SU) requires a combination of insight—the ability to accurately perceive an existing situation—and foresight—the ability to anticipate how an existing situation may develop in the future."[3] Absent the ability to master these skills, one is left with a shallow understanding that translates into a weak or ill-prepared plan.

4 & 5. CONSIDERATION OF ALTERNATIVES
AND ACTION TIMELINES

Alternatives and *action timelines* are inextricably linked; although they are separate factors in the planning process, they must be considered together, as a timeline is crucial in considering the critical path for any activity or action. This is especially true for construction in the field of education, as many construction-type projects are planned for the summer period between school years or other periods when students are not present, such as winter and spring breaks.

When developing plans, one of the most important elements is that of consideration of alternatives, options, and other ways of getting to the same result. "There's more than one way of achieving one's aim." This expression advises us to realize the importance of options and consideration of which option is best suited to accomplish our goals. The basic meaning is, there is more than one way to do that. So let's pick one and do this thing! Hold on there. Selection of an alternative is not to be confused with a call to action. In the case of Josh Lucas, popular movie actor, telling us to get off our butts and tackle those home projects in the recent Home Depot ad campaign, "Let's Do This!" or Nike's "Just Do It"—OK fine, but *how* and with *what*? Each example provides a plethora of options and choices, from grades and finishes with Home Depot to athletic foot gear and training regimens with Nike.

In business we must limit the probability of failure or excessive cash layout by eliminating potential barriers and reducing avoidable delays that center on two of our most precious resources, *time* and *money*.

Timelines are critical in allowing planning to work. They provide structure and order to assist in tracking and checking of progress. Linear in nature they help us to move from point "A" to "B" on our pathway to "C"—completion. Timelines are integral in visualizing our success in overall goal attainment by recording completion of tasks and objectives along the way.

While they can be vertical or horizontal, they share two common traits: they are measurable and reflect order of events or sequencing.

In business we utilize timelines for a number of activities, such as budget, purchasing, projects, event planning, and financial tracking. Timelines tell stories, help us analyze and digest occurrences, measure progress and visualize success, and develop activities, such as changes, throughout a given period.

One activity in business that relies heavily on timelines is construction. Construction timelines are typically produced and reflected in Gantt charts (bar charts that depict work completed over time) that help us visualize the progress of each trade over the project life cycle. It is imperative to ensure the general contractor (GC) and all subcontractors are adhering to the schedule, thus ensuring critical milestones within the overall schedule are being met.

6 & 7. FLEXIBILITY AND STRATEGIES

Flexibility allows us to maneuver and adjust to any number of factors that are currently present and potential challenges that come during the implementation stage. Flexibility in planning is what allows us to *pivot, adapt, improvise,* and *overcome* factors, such as shifts in the labor market, changes in supply and demand, market conditions, consumer confidence, resource availability, and cash flow, all of which require contingencies. If we remain rigid, we cannot proceed once we see a curve in the road and would surely lose control or momentum by slamming on the brakes.

In a 2017 article that appeared in Entrepreneur.com, flexibility was called out as vital to success now more than ever:

> In today's competitive environment of technology-fueled 24/7 marketing, we also need to be flexible. Gone are the days where we can create business and marketing plans a year ahead of time and expect them to be etched in stone. Sure, planning is a necessity, particularly for long-term vision, positioning and innovation, but just as important is short-term activity. Movement is key, and responsiveness drives movement.[4]

The article goes on to state, "flexibility has taken on a pivotal role in decision making"[5] through new data, emerging target audiences (millennials), and shifts in business models, referring to the demise of brick-and-mortar stores. This reality will be explored further in chapter 9.

Strategies allow planning to include activities that are focused on organizational priorities that strengthen and improve overall operations. They keep us on track in obtaining desired outcomes.

The most successful organizations maintain a set of focus areas to ensure alignment of organizational activities and actions with organizational goals over a given period, typically three years. They form the foundation of strategic planning. In a blog post, "Creating Focus Areas," the point is underscored by saying, "Focus areas are the foundation stones of your strategy. They expand on your Vision Statement and start to create some structure around how to actually get your organization to achieve its goals."[6]

One question referenced in the article is, how many focus areas should an organization have? Not only a good question but one that many organizations ponder. I have found three to four meaningful focus areas serve as a great aim in as much as you need to ensure they work to guide the organization in all aspects of decision-making, communications, investment, organizational practices, policy-making, and stakeholder engagement for that time period.

Too few, and you may narrow the group's focus into a tunnel vision; too many, and you could develop competing interests that stretch available

resources too thin as well as creating confusion as to the actual desired outcomes. This could in turn lead to an identity crisis leaving those within the organization uncertain as to what the vision really is or what the focus should be.

In my own organization we utilize a three-year model of three focus areas
derived from various stakeholder meetings that give enough time for thought,
input, and free exchange of priorities based on our particular needs. For this
very reason a needs assessment is pivotal to creation of common goals that
are bolstered by authentic focus areas. *Focus areas created without honest
input and feedback from your stakeholders are not only disruptive; they become an empty exercise with no benefit.* Done properly, they allow us to align
the *vision* with *mission* in a way that guarantees the organization's success.

ESSENTIALS FOR DEVELOPING STRATEGIC FOCUS AREAS

To ensure meaningful development of strategic focus areas we need to establish meaningful criteria. The following five principles act as a guide to assist
you in the process:

1. **Authenticity**: The process must exude the quality and condition of being
   authentic, trustworthy, or genuine.
2. **Brevity**: Each focus area should be concise, short enough to become actionable.
3. **Clarity**: Be clear in establishing the expectations or desired outcomes.
   Avoid wordsmithing, as this sometimes acts as a ploy by the minority to
   avoid what was originally intended by the majority.
4. **Functionality**: Each focus area should be deep enough to have value and
   meaning yet functional enough to be put into practice.
5. **Simplicity**: Use plain language that is easily understood by all stakeholders and members of your organization who will be tasked to carry it out.

When creating organizational focus areas, avoid getting bogged down in
metrics or specific targets; they are reserved for goals and objectives. The
process needs to be facilitated by applying a higher-level thinking approach.

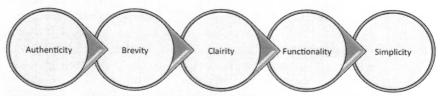

Figure 2.2.   Five Principles of Developing Strategic Focus Areas

The "30,000-foot view" is a common business phrase used to describe getting a high-level view to see the big picture. It is exactly the right approach for development of focus areas. Stepping back and *looking broad* allows for a shift in perspective. Perspective defines how we see the things in our personal lives, our work, and the world in which we live. It forms our beliefs and cements our reality of how things are and therefore what needs to be done to properly address, change, and improve things—our point of view. Seeing someone else's point of view becomes difficult the more entrenched you become with your own, unless of course it is aligned with or similar to your own. The problem with this perspective is you limit your exposure by shutting off other opportunities to see things differently, thus restricting your view to those who think like you. That kills off creativity and leaves the experience lacking. *The world changes when we change our perspective.*

Another pitfall to avoid in creating focus areas is a push for instant accountability in the language, thus restricting the flow of big ideas by interjecting metrics. A propensity to add metrics in the development of focus areas is usually supported with one word or some derivative of that word—data. Whether the conversation veers toward inclusion of "data analysis" or "data analytics," it often springs from those intent on whipping out the measuring stick to guard against lofty and spirited sentiments that become unobtainable or elusive goals or pipe dreams. That is why clarity is so important along with specificity.

Keep in mind, at this point we are not talking about development of goals; we must however remain mindful of the goals when developing the focus areas. While this is not the time or place for metrics, they are important and critical in the assessment phase of progress toward goal attainment. As we widen the lens of a camera, we are able to capture a bigger picture.

Development of our goals and focus areas is enhanced by organizing team activities or wide area planning, such as community or stakeholder forums. This allows us to design our road maps to success that are customized based on our specific needs. All messaging needs to align with the focus and vision for consistency and purpose and to ensure directional outcomes are reached.

The importance of getting quality feedback and input during this process requires multiple meetings with time for reflection and consumption on key ideas and communications around the process. If done too quickly, the process gives off the appearance of lack of effort, seriousness, or substance, and the outcomes become questionable.

Chapter Three

Directional Planning "Logistics"

You Are Here (Determining Position)

Where are we going? What needs to be done? How do we get there? These are all directional questions that your team leaders (executives, managers, and supervisors) will need to articulate and disseminate in various ways as part of the organization's logistical planning to ensure they are moving in the right direction—at the right pace—while pursuing the goals in furtherance of the mission.

We are all familiar with the Latin phrase "Carpe diem," or "seize the day!" However, before we can seize that day, we need to get a line in it, or as the Romans would say, "None dei sine linea," meaning "no day without a plan." An azimuth lets us plot that line in any given direction. In order to plot the line, we need to know which way is up, or in this case true north, as azimuths are calculated in a clockwise manner. A back azimuth allows us to look back to our point of origin and measure how far we have traveled. This is crucial in telling our story and graphing our progress through linear graphs or timelines denoting minor and major victories and challenges conquered along the way. "The azimuth is the most common military method to express direction. When using an azimuth, the point from which the azimuth originates is the center of an imaginary circle."[1]

So before we start to plan we must answer the most important question— where are we?

Being in the right place at the prescribed time is necessary to successfully accomplish military missions. From drop zones to rally points, from grid coordinates to targets, the military relies on maps and timelines to carry out logistics of troop movements in a wide variety of initiatives and campaigns.

As stated in the army field manual on map reading and land navigation,[2] direction plays an important role in a soldier's everyday life. It can be expressed as right, left, straight ahead, and so forth, but then the question arises, "To the right of what?"

Without map skills a soldier can miss the rally point, arrive at the wrong objective, arrive late, engage the wrong target, or miss the LZ (landing zone) and be left behind. While mapping is critical to the success of the military and has been for centuries, more businesses and organizations today are recognizing and depending on some of these basic transferable skills to navigate their own challenging landscapes to ensure they are not left behind.

Directional planning is developing a road map to success. In education we have adopted the term *mapping* to ensure our students achieve the desired outcomes that we expect in order to ensure they master the competencies needed to achieve in the 21st century. As organizations we need to adopt similar mapping skills to ensure our own success and achievement of our desired outcomes—that of reaching our goals.

"From the very beginning of mapmaking, maps have been made for some particular purpose or set of purposes."[3]

Webster's defines cartography[4] as the science or art of making maps; Wikipedia goes a step further, defining it as "The study and practice of making maps. Combining science, aesthetics, and technique, cartography builds on the premise that reality can be modeled in ways that communicate spatial information effectively."[5] In reality it is a skill that allowed once masters of the roadways, like Rand McNally, Hagstrom, and AAA, to guide us on road trips, vacations, and business trips, as they produced paper maps of regions, counties, and states to ensure we got where we needed to go.

Maps back then were just as necessary as they are today, although most have gone the way of the wastebasket, as digital devices with mapping technology have all but replaced paper maps. Most cartography companies have all but vanished over the past thirty years, and even those still around, like Rand McNally, have adapted to changing market conditions with travel-related software and online map and travel content. According to the company profile on Dun & Bradstreet's Business Directory, they also make GPS devices and routing navigation software for the commercial transportation industry (IntelliRoute) as well as fleet-management software (TruckPC).[6] This serves as a good example of a company's ability to adjust in planning to remain relevant, as their future was not as certain in January 2003 when the company was acquired by Leonard Green & Partners through a chapter 11 restructuring deal after falling behind the technology curve of upstarts, such as MapQuest, at the time (1990s).[7]

Although the medium has changed, how maps are produced and provided—our reliance on maps is more than ever—as GPS has become a part of each person's daily life. Maps are now more accessible and easier than ever to follow with turn-by-turn instructions to help us get where we need to go, from long journeys to city walks through highly congested building areas.

Road maps are strategic in planning, as they take us to our goals or desired outcomes through various routes that mark our progress as we travel to those points.

A good map is one in which the user can easily follow, understand and chart a course that leads them to their destination along the fastest route in a safe manner while navigating the road ahead and the terrain they must travel. The same is true for businesses today, and as managers, we need mapping skills to navigate and lead our teams down the right roads and avoid wrong turns, hazards, and dead ends.

This is accomplished by using key tools found in the map's legend. The legend gives you the key information needed for the map to make sense. It breaks things down through use of color and symbols to provide clarity, focus, and direction in the way it differentiates between local roads, county roads, state highways, and interstates or toll roads all the while ensuring direction with a standard use of north as the top of the map orientation along with scale to provide measurement for distance to your target(s). Not all maps produced are considered good maps; if the traveler was unable to ascertain these basic elements from the map, then the map may be rendered useless.

So how do we begin mapping our success within our own organizations? It starts with the most basic map skill—*orientation*. Orienting ourselves to the map accomplishes this by recognizing objects, terrain, and landmarks. We need to know where we are before we can begin plotting any course, even if we know the destination. That starts with assessment.

Think about all the assessments a company or organization has available to assist with this task. It is needed in order to gain valuable insight into who they are (identity), what they have (resources), and where they want to be (positioning). This can easily be accomplished through a SWOT analysis—strengths, weaknesses, opportunities, and threats—or online assessment software tools that generate personalized feedback reports.

But let's dig deeper. In addition to organizational assessment tools, such as outside consultants, market analysis (if publicly traded), rankings, surveys, consumer satisfaction, and a plethora of data, from income statements to profit and loss statements, quarterly reports, annual reports, or any other relevant data used to determine profitability and overall value—we must focus within the organization itself. These are all global approaches to assess the company from the outside (external). What about taking the temperature from within? Other ways to go beyond the overall assessment is to look within through managerial tools that take the pulse of the organization and find out *why we do what we do* and more importantly *can we do it better*.

There are a number of types of management assessment tools, such as employee feedback, retreats, 360-degree assessments, and self-assessments for various audiences to include executives, managers, teams, and individuals. Likewise, many source providers of these tools are available online at sites, such as *hoganassessments.com*, *surveyanyplace.com*, and *thinkwiseinc.com* to guide your employees with clear, actionable reports that add value to the overall process.

One of the most impactful organizational tools still utilized today is the Myers–Briggs Type Indicator (MBTI) personality inventory. When first introduced to this assessment I remember going into it with a varying degree of interest, as I knew what my management style and type was before I got the results (ESTJ). What I didn't know and what blew me away was what my colleagues were and why I got along with some better than others. That is the key in the Myers–Briggs assessments; it teaches you how to interact in more productive ways with those around you who perceive things differently.

Now that we've looked at external assessment tools as well as internal assessment tools, we must protect against blind spots with blind spot assessments. In navigating our field of business while traveling through our sector, we must also be looking at the blind spots and blind spot assessments that provide the same safety for our businesses as the blind spot technology equipped in most cars provide for their passengers.

Blind spots are seen by others as character or leadership flaws that hold back good executives and managers from being great leaders. They have nothing to do with ability, skill, drive, or determination, all of which got most high-level executives to where they are within those organizations. Instead, they have to do with personal interaction with others within your organization and outside of it as well. Depending on how intense the negative actions (blind spots) become if left unaddressed, they could bring down the organization itself.

In most cases even if mildly ignored, the negative ramifications are felt by staff and other managers within the organization, thus creating unnecessary friction, distrust, and apathy during the day-to-day operations, which ultimately hampers morale and productivity.

In an Inc.com January 2019 article, CEO Peter Bregman writes, "Uncovering your blind spots is hard. Every leader must ask themselves these two questions."[8] Those question are part of the feedback process to determine your personal strengths and weaknesses in how you operate and how you are perceived by those around you and often those closest to you on a daily basis.

1. "What do I do that helps me, you, our team, and the organization succeed?"[9]

2. "What do I do that makes it harder for me, you, our team, and the organization to succeed?"[10]

Anyone in a leadership position who has done this finds it to be about as pleasant of an experience as getting a root canal but just as effective in relieving the long-term pain of ignoring the problem. Conjures up one term for me that hits the mark—*courageous conversations*.

Finding those available with the heart, courage, and true concern to voice the honest assessment is rare but achievable as long as the leaders can listen without threat of reprisals.

As an organization this is important to the mission in that, as we plan, we need to ensure those representing us are able to lead in the way and direction needed to move the organization to our destination.

Many common dangers in the form of blind spot characteristics can be grouped into three distinct area deficiencies: operational, leadership, and interpersonal.

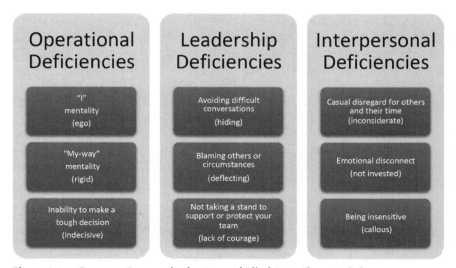

Figure 3.1.   Common Dangers in the Form of Blind Spot Characteristics

Once the orientation process is complete and we have acquired our grid coordinates (*where we are*) and we have determined our goals (*where we want to go*), we need to plan our objectives (*travel routes*). This is where our next map skill comes into play—determination of *scale* to properly size the representations to reality and *distance* to measure how far we must travel. Again, like any good map, we must provide our teams with metrics to determine what is necessary to properly equip those teams for the journey. As managers and leaders it is our responsibility to ensure our organizations are ready to go the distance. This means ensuring they are properly trained, equipped, and prepared to travel the routes determined in the planning stage.

Simply put—we must make every effort to guarantee success in the achievement of our objectives to fulfill the attainment of our goals.

Scale is required to navigate maps correctly—it allows one to accurately understand the distance of various routes. Other major activities that affect us are also measured in scale, like tornados (Fujita scale), earthquakes (Richter scale), and hurricanes (Saffir–Simpson scale). In this case the purpose of the scale is to allow us to plan accordingly, and based on those measurements, allow us to quickly ascertain size, impact, and potential damage, which in turn drives our decision-making with respect to scale of preparation.

While not as dramatic, the scale of any map is equally important to ensure we gauge the distances properly prior to heading off to our destination. Similar to the above reference to extreme weather, again the purpose of the scale is to allow us to plan accordingly, and based on these measurements, allow us to quickly ascertain distance, time, and resources required to make the trip.

Distance requires measurement and as such requires a baseline or starting point referred to in military map reading as zero measure or point of reference.[11] Again, the purpose of determining zero measure or the baseline is transferable to organizations. You must first establish a baseline in order to graph and chart progress, or lack thereof, based on the determination of the x- and y-axes. The measurement between two points allows us to consider the distance as long as we have an accurate scale. The farther the points lie from one another, the longer the distance; however, without scale we are unable to determine the true distance and therefore unable to plan accordingly. Keep in mind when developing your scale that it should be realistic, meaningful, and accurate so as not to skew the results or camouflage underlying concerns, referred to as *manipulating the scale.*

Think about the long trips you have taken and all the planning that takes place, in contrast to short drives where you just start the car and go. On a long trip you probably get the car serviced in the weeks prior to the trip, ensuring all fluids are topped off to avoid breakdowns, which lead to delays. Let's not forget about filling the tank, as we typically gas up the night before the big start so we can get out early to beat the traffic. Scale is used to determine mileage and thus hours of driving time to plan for breaks, meals, and lodging.

Now, think about your own organization and the resources available, including human resources to make the trips (objectives) on your journey to reach the ultimate destination (goals, both short and long term). Is there enough "gas in the tank"? If not, you may find your company broken down on the side of the road or arriving to market a bit late with no vacancies available.

Another aid in our travels are road signs telling us everything from directions—to speed limits—to warnings—to rest stops—and even where to exit for food, gas, and lodging. Let's face it; they are helpful communication tools that are needed. Strategically placed, they provide the right guidance and information at the right time. In the case of exits, they are usually a mile ahead of the actual event to allow us time to process and plan accordingly, based on changes in our needs or unanticipated stops.

Companies and organizations that run successfully are also effective at utilizing signs (communication tools) to provide information for actions that need to be taken. Instead of along the road they may be closer to the water cooler, on electronic bulletin boards or shared in email blasts. They come in the form of emails, memos, letters, bulletins, notices, updates, and advisories. While each serves a different purpose and some are forwarded from external sources, including local, state, and federal agencies for adherence to laws and regulations, they serve the same purpose—to allow you time to process and plan accordingly, based on changes in needs.

Lastly, we need to understand the terrain in which we must navigate in business as with travel. This requires an understanding of the *field* we compete on and an industry outlook that includes our competitors, rivals, and partners along with a *history of the past, understanding of the present*, and *focus on the future* through research, analysis, and projections.

Basically getting the lay of the land, or as we referred to it in the military, a "topo map," or topographic map. These maps portray terrain features in a measurable way as well as horizontal and vertical positions of representations with contour lines. Architects and engineers utilize these type of maps exclusively in the planning stages of projects or undertaking site work involving surveying, grading, excavation, drainage, and foundations or determining design layouts for roads, parking lots, sidewalks, and retaining walls. They too must be on point and sure of direction in order to get where they need to be—successful completion of the project in order to attain their goal—payment.

Now that we see the value and benefit of mapping for organizations in getting from point A to B, let's apply it to process. Regardless of the type of organization you are a part of, we all experience process in unique ways that belongs to each organization. Process represents the way organizations *do things*, although many of our means and methods go unassessed as to the value add each activity has or the overall ROI (return on investment) for each program. In order to begin understanding and analyzing *what we do* and *how we do it*, we must understand and reflect on it through use of tools, such as charts, graphs, and data analysis. Organizational charts for instance provide us with a graphical representation of an organization's structure—how it is broken down and how reporting responsibilities work both up and down the chart (chain of command). The tool illustrates the reporting relationships and chains of command in a quick, easy visual that aids in understanding where people and departments fit within the overall structure. This is especially true of large organizations with multiple levels.

Work flow diagrams are just as helpful in understanding and mapping out processes we use for critical tasks to carry out our business. They communicate how a process works or how it should work if the operation is running according to plan. By creating a pictorial of the process (visual) we can better review and analyze easier. It allows us to streamline any processes within the organization that we see to be less productive or inefficient.

"Workflows help employees keep track of the tasks (or) steps in the process. With a visual layout telling them what needs to be done, when, and by whom, cumulative delays are less likely. Looking from a broad top-down perspective of everyday operations at your organization, you can identify potential bottlenecks, flaws in process guidelines, and areas that can be improved."[12]

Today, there are many online tools and web-based programs to assist with these elements of holistic planning. Lucidchart is one example of an online web-based proprietary platform that allows users to collaborate on drawing, revising, and sharing charts and diagrams within their organization. With a mission of *helping millions connect the dots and bring big ideas to life,* they allow one to create a visual workspace that combines diagramming, data visualization, and collaboration to accelerate understanding and drive innovation.[13]

While each chart type discussed has different purposes with respect to chain of command and process, they work together to provide the answers to *What needs to be done?* and *How do we get there?* Through use of mapping skills, assessments, data analysis, and effective communications, we can apply logistics in a way that gives us control over directional planning.

Chapter Four

Alignment

Aligning the Vision with the Mission

Strategic Vision Management (SVM) is a clear and focused way to *align the vision with the mission* in any organization. This begins with development of a strategic plan that lays out the end goals and how to achieve them. SVM is about making decisions today that will have an impact on our future in a way that makes our vision actionable—seeing things not as they are but how they can become.

My first recollection of this was in 2002 when the executive director of New Jersey Association of School Business Officials (NJASBO) brought forward a vision of increased educational requirements for all school business administrators in New Jersey. As a member of the education committee, we were tasked with exploring ways to add value to our membership in support of this vision. Through the leadership of the executive director and members of the executive committee it was brought to the committee for discussion and creation of actionable steps. That meant raising the professional standards for school business leaders across the state.

Working with the New Jersey Department of Education State Certification Office, we decided in order to raise the bar for attainment of the necessary state certification or licensing for school business administrator we would require a master's degree. At the time the majority of our membership possessed a bachelor's degree in business administration or accounting or held a CPA (Certified Public Accountant) license.

While many of the committee members had already attained the master's degree with some in possession of an MBA, there were those at the time, like me, who would then be "grandfathered" and thus not required to attain the advanced degree, as we already held the standard certificate for the position. In the committee there were some who lacked the vision and were content to remain with the status quo. They argued a different position which placed less of an importance on the educational requirements for success in the position. They lost that argument, as the requirement was recommended to the trustees, then ratified by the association and shortly thereafter adopted into the official prerequisites by the licensure board.

In the example above with the education requirements of a master's degree in New Jersey for SBAs—while the situation is unique to this particular organization, the concept is applicable to any organization. The *vision train*, in this case called *higher educational standards*, was leaving the station with those on board either grandfathered or already meeting the new criteria. However, any aspiring SBAs who wanted *to board* needed to *get their ticket*, in this case, a master's degree, to ride that train or be left at the depot holding their bachelor's degree. Recognizing that *vision*, I made it *my mission* to attain an MBA in finance in 2005 to stay current, marketable, and in line with my peers.

Vision and mission are difficult for many people to discern—what is the difference? It is this: "Without vision any mission is directionless and simply a waste of time, money and effort."

Then as with now, I find it ironic that anyone could not see the vision of our executive director and the executive committee in pursing this long-term outlook for our organization of raising the bar, with higher educational requirements, since we work in the field of education.

It came up in discussions this summer (2019) during a NJASBO meeting held at the headquarters in Robbinsville, New Jersey. The discussion centered on comments regarding the challenge of attracting new comers to the profession. A couple of business administrators questioned the continued need for the master's degree, as they saw it as a potential barrier to entry into the management level of school business operations. They further suggested perhaps, if we lowered the requirements we would attract greater numbers of interested candidates who possessed a bachelor's degree in business administration or accounting. After some brief discussion it became clear to the group that the steps taken in 2002 were instrumental in ensuring that the qualifications, knowledge, and exposure of graduate-level coursework was in fact needed to attain success in the position. As the profession has only become more rigorous over the past twenty years with increasingly more demands on the various responsibilities of the office it was felt the importance of having the master's was now more than ever.

Additionally, it was made clear that there is a direct correlation between the educational training level of an advanced degree and the prestige and respect the holders of the position enjoy as professional CFOs. In managing operations for public school districts, that challenge is equivalent to private industry with small, midsize, and large companies, with many districts operating budgets over $100 million. Needless to say, the conversation was short and the understanding of the need to continue the requirements of the advanced degree was maintained by the rest of the group.

Michigan University's Executive Education program informs prospective students, "Your effectiveness as a senior leader is measured by the performance of the leaders you manage. They rely on your ability to align, inspire, and drive business results."[1]

By *aligning the vision with the mission,* we ensure our efforts in any planning phase allow for success on a larger scale by directing our efforts and employing our resources in a manner that equates *desired outcomes* with actual results thus transforming them into *strategic outcomes.*

"Effective educational leaders develop, advocate, and enact a shared mission, vision, and core values of high-quality education and academic success and well-being of each student."[2]

In an online article hosted by ProSky, a task-oriented company providing predictive intelligence for hiring managers and human capital professionals, Hannah Son lays it out in three sentences, "Every company needs to have a vision. As a leader, it is your job to create this vision and make it known. Without a vision, your company is like someone swimming circles in the ocean and bound to sink eventually."[3]

The article goes on to talk about getting people in your organization to realize that vision by making sure they are all on the same page.

Sounds great—so how do we accomplish that task? Start with planning!

Keep in mind—the bigger the company the bigger the task. Everything we do must connect back to our vision, *the plan for our future*, and what we are in the process of doing, *our current mission.*

That vision needs to be embedded into the fabric of your organization's processes beginning with the hiring process as part of the expectations to ensure a proper fit and solidified in the norming process through onboarding, "make sure your employees are aware of the vision from day one."[4]

To truly master this concept, we need to ensure our teams experience it and live it day in and day out as part of the organizational identity that separates us from other like organizations in a way that is special and appreciated. That breeds loyalty which in turn develops trust, pride, and a sense of belonging, which leads to longevity and higher retention rates.

Creating a strategic plan may be the first step; however, keeping that plan alive and in force is the real test. Perry Soldwedel, director of Programs and Services for the Consortium for Educational Change in Springfield, Illinois, and Brett Clark, director of Communications for Maine Township High School in Park Ridge, Illinois, address this challenge facing school districts, citing turnover at the top of the organization as a real problem.[5]

They point out many reasons that strategic plans get pushed aside, from changes in leadership at the top level, referring to superintendents, also referred to as chief school administrators (CSAs) or CEOs, and board members, who act in the same capacity as board of directors in the private sector. Longevity in these positions is key to achievement of long-term vision, as many impactful goals are multiyear goals requiring a constant and steady approach in attainment. When key individuals within the team leave, we can lose time, focus, and energy in retraining or renorming new arrivals; however, when those at the top leave in the middle of the campaign we often see a delay of a year or more, and sometimes a total new plan emerges as the new CEO, or in this case, superintendent may have their own vision, which looks nothing like that of their predecessor.

The article goes on to list six other factors,[6] including failure to report or monitor the plan and, more concerning, *nonalignment of the vision with the budget or the necessary prioritization of adequate resources for implementation.*[7]

Whenever the budget is out of alignment with the vision, we are simply spending money with no regard for the plan. Not only is that irresponsible—it is dangerous. Chief executives and directors who ignore this basic function (*fiscal management*) are setting up the organization for failure and, even worse, turning their vision into a risky proposition that may leave the organization's financial health on life support with depleted reserves and increased infusions of cash needed.

"When planning is approached as a budgeting exercise, there can be a tendency to fill in the numbers on a spreadsheet based on a mindset that says, the people are in place, other costs are givens, the work is what it is, so here's the number for next year."[8]

This is truly worrisome, as it lacks thought, direction, and review of what is at stake (the mission) and where we are going (the vision).

"High-performing companies budget, too, of course, but they use the planning process to give them something more: a springboard for identifying and evaluating new opportunities, considering new strategies, and discussing objectives that may at first seem unattainable."[9]

Unfortunately, many leaders realize this too late, and, at that point, not only is their vision impacted; their tenure with the organization is in jeopardy. This creates a mess for all involved, as the board is left to deal with the fallout, including a loss of confidence, need for damage control, and installation of a new leader with a new vision. Even if the vision does not change, the setback is costly and may take years in the making for any viable or attainable comeback as the group needs to regain trust.

The same goes for missions that are taken up on a whim or at someone else's direction in the organization that is flying solo or following a separate vision. This can happen out of resentment of the plan or vision, operational silos that are disconnected from the vision, poor or lacking communications of the vision, or lack of oversight to enforce the vision.

Strategic plans that encompass the organizational vision are not strategic at all if that vision is not properly aligned with the mission. Just the opposite—they are in fact out of alignment and therefore *short lived* once the realization sets in that the organizational resources, whether they be the necessary manpower, adequately trained personnel, or physical assets required to sustain the mission, are lacking. That requires discipline and execution. Keeping strategic plans alive requires both. McChesney, Covey, and Hauling address this in their book—*4 Disciplines of Execution*:[10] focus, leverage, engagement, and accountability.

1. The *discipline of focus*—Be clear about what matters most.
2. The *discipline of leverage*—Put energy toward measures that are predictive of goal attainment.
3. The *discipline of engagement*—Create a compelling dashboard or data system to focus on as you act.
4. The *discipline of accountability*—Create a system of accountability that requires holding one another accountable for goal actions and results.

Lacking discipline, execution becomes a futile exercise that strips us of our resources while producing confusion and leaving us ill-prepared to navigate new challenges or take on new missions in pursuit of our goals. Again, drafting the "best" strategic plan on paper is a wasted exercise if that plan cannot be realized or implemented. Leaders must ensure they are conducting a proper and realistic inventory in drafting the goals and considering the mission before finalizing any strategic plan.

Just going through the exercise as an annual obligation, either drafting a new plan or reviewing the existing plan, wastes time, energy, and focus.

"Depending on which study you follow; the statistics range from a dismal 3% of companies whose executives say they are successful at executing their strategies to at best about one out of every three organizations that integrates its plans into its daily operations with high effectiveness."[11]

A healthy strategic plan is one that not only starts with proper alignment (SVM); it must be developed in a collaborative framework of synergy to incorporate our processes, procedures, and talents. It is one that requires ongoing focus and attention through periodic review and daily implementation. Like any worthwhile activity we need to ensure integration at every level

within the organization with an eye on the vision and a mindset of implementation and integration of the mission. *This is how we keep it authentic,
actionable, and relative—this is how we keep it real!* Failure to do this leads
to abandonment or deviation from the vision, taking us further from the desire
outcomes of our plan.

Finally, we must guard against too many initiatives, goals, or expected
outcomes. Think about the shows of late on cable TV designed to rescue businesses from themselves. *Bar Rescue,*[12] *Hotel Impossible,*[13] and *Restaurant
Impossible.*[14] These shows are all about one thing, besides ratings and viewer-
ship; they promote basic business fundamentals, such as planning, managing,
and utilization of available resources.

A central message throughout the shows is to reduce the services or offerings on the menu, as they provide too many choices, options, or variety,
resulting in less than excellent quality and customer satisfaction. Instead, the
managers are encouraged to strip the choices down to a core of high-quality
offerings that ensure the expected experience is achieved. The shows are all
successful in promoting one very simple yet important message—*stick to
what you do best and limit your activities to match your available resources.*

Strategy Vision Management (SVM) is all about delivering a *high-quality
product* in a way that ensures you stand out in the marketplace by exceeding
expectations. It is about developing a strategy that joins our vision with our
mission in a way that *adds value* by combining three distinct ingredients:
Mission—Vision—Value (MV²).

Once we have this accomplished we can begin to build plans around that
vision utilizing the development of SMART goals, use of key performance
indicators (KPI) to track the progress, and budget integration to exercise the
discipline of planning. Lastly, we need to ensure the progress is ongoing and
the goals are met.

None of this happens without a strategic plan; however, just developing the
plan does not guarantee attainment of our goals. It is a process and as such
requires multiple steps in positioning, development, planning, and management. The basic elements or steps are summarized in Figure 4.1.

While alignment is critical to the overall health and success of the vision, it
is not reached quickly or without some pain. It requires adjustments of various parts of the organization in the same way a chiropractor works to align
the spine by alignment of the hips, back, and neck. The CEO must work in
tandem with other members of the executive team, directors, and supervisors
in probing and questioning the processes. They must look at the structure, responsibilities, and effectiveness of each department, section, and area within
the organization to fully ascertain the strengths, weaknesses, opportunities,
and threats. This must be done before any alignments with respect to mission

Figure 4.1. Steps in the Strategic Planning Process

and vision to ensure they are truly in sync, or the vision is simply a quest that will never be truly realized.

EmployeeConnect, an Australian HR software company and a leading industry provider of innovative solutions, supports this concept stating, "While a lot of employees truly wish their company to succeed, the fact remains that these best intentions need to be properly aligned to connect them to your organization's mission."[15] This requires investing the proper time in development of your mission, narrowing your vision to see clearly, communicating your values, and aligning your team with that mission.

This is *how we do it*, this is *why we do it*, and this is *how you succeed* in developing a strategic plan that ensures alignment of the *vision* with *mission*.

Part II

THE VALUE OF PLANNING

Chapter Five

Holistic Planning

While we have already touched on holistic planning with SMART goals, focus areas, and alignment of employees with the vision and the mission, we have not gone deep enough to provide purpose, meaning, and value. Quite simply it is planning in a holistic or all-encompassing manner that ensures all the parts of the organization are gelling as they set to become more solid.

When a leader of any team, company, or organization claims to have their finger on the pulse of that team, company, organization, or client base and yet they cannot answer questions beyond the basics regarding the operations—they are in trouble. Just having the overview of the structure (organizational chart), company bio, or any other information available to the public or outsiders does not constitute a detailed knowledge of the organization at all.

Information taken from an annual report, company profile, or audit is good for familiarization, analysis, and comparisons to other companies in the same field or sector of the market; however, it does not equate to a deep knowledge of that company. It is still *outside* information provided by *insiders* who have the details.

A company's mission, history, and achievements can be gleaned from a brochure in the company's lobby or website. This type of information is helpful to potential investors, especially the financials and market share information along with long-range outlooks. It is all outbound information designed to draw new investors in and keep existing investors interested as well as reporting to stakeholders of the company or organization, including nonprofits.

What it *doesn't do*, what it *can't do*, is provide the *skinny*, or inside information on the real health of the company or organization. Oftentimes, companies are in trouble long before the stock reports or financials come out. By the time the financials or other indicators are released, a cancer can be spreading that all but guts the very company that those leaders, who had their finger on the pulse, are now strapping on their parachute and heading for the door.

Too often we see CEOs of major companies, superintendents of school districts, or executive directors of organizations leave only to find out after their departure that the companies and organizations left behind are in serious trouble, whether it be financial, budgetary, or mismanagement. In some cases, those individuals at the top that are "bailing out" are good people who just weren't good leaders—leaders who failed to plan effectively. Just because individuals advance or obtain higher leadership positions, it doesn't always mean that they will become great leaders. And when accountability is lacking, from a governance responsibility, the damage can go on longer and go deeper.

Real detail and deep understanding is achieved only by being *involved*, *present*, and *aware* of critical indicators, such as operational efficiency, employee morale, budgetary challenges, and clear insight into the development of the strategic plan. Leaders who have this—have the pulse of the organization and therefore the ability to create—maintain and support both the *vision* and the *mission*.

So how do we get this understanding and achieve this presence? Think of it as an *organizational walkabout*. Unlike the Australian Aboriginal journey into the wilderness for a period of up to six months, these walkabouts can be short, targeted, and accomplished within minutes or hours spread out over time. To ensure this happens you need insist that executives, directors, and managers get out of their offices and into the operations of your organization whether that be schools and classrooms in education, the floor in manufacturing, or departments and back rooms in retail.

Holistic planning is a broad exercise involving all aspects of the organization to plan in tandem, thus ensuring each area of the operation is included in the planning of all exercises. Regardless of the degree or role they play in each plan, each department must be involved for the planning to be truly holistic. That does not mean they need to be in every meeting, briefing, or conference; nevertheless, they should be aware of what was discussed and decisions resulting from those meetings where any major initiatives that are planned. This can be easily accomplished through email, memos, or bulletins. This is not only keeping them in the loop; it is smart business sense, as it allows other departments and supervisors to do a better job of support once they understand what they are supporting.

Organizations plan at every level and in differing degrees; however, by working together in the broader exercise they ensure the greater success of the company or organization as a whole. One department's task may be to provide support for another department for a brief time while they work on a specific project. Other departments may have a continual mission of support for another group within the operation and therefore need to know about any changes in that department (major or minor) in order to continue to provide optimal support.

Holistic planning impacts every department and all individuals to differing degrees, depending on the role they play in any particular plan, whether it be logistics, budget, resource management, human relations, purchasing, or any variety of functional needs that ensure the company or organization remains mission driven.

"High-performance organizations are linked to being mission-driven companies."[1]

When you think about "holistic planning," think about the spokes on a wheel; they each represent components of the company or organization with groups, larger or smaller, representing bands within the organization that make up departments, sections, divisions, and so on, depending on the size of the company. Each spoke serves to provide strength to the outer rim. As such each spoke is critical to the integrity of the company or, in this example, the wheel.

Spokes are the connecting rods between the hub (core) and the rim (support). Their main purpose is to transfer the loads between the hub and the rim. Holistic planning is taking into account each spoke by alignment of the bands in a way that reduces the overall load on the total company. This ensures the needed strength to the perimeter or the organization's health.

If we are not planning holistically, then we begin to compromise or weaken the overall wheel, as the rim becomes susceptible to damage and begins to fail. Now, any company can still run missing a few spokes, even in a compromised position. It will, however, eventually break down and, depending on the number of spokes that become compromised, such as a major strand (department or group), fail faster.

Holistic planning requires us to master the art of planning. *Collins English Dictionary* defines a master plan as, "A clever plan that is intended to help someone succeed in a very difficult or important task."[2]

Throughout history one of the most deserved holders of the title *master planner* belongs to Alexander Hamilton. He was the quintessential achiever—driven, creative, and optimistic. He had the ability to influence those around him to join his causes and accomplish his goals, which were large, ambitious, and meaningful.

In the summer of 1788, he served as a delegate to the New York Ratifying Convention in Poughkeepsie and helped convince largely antifederalist New York to ratify the new constitution. Historians report of his ability to work with others in furtherance of any cause, evidenced by joining James Madison and John Jay in writing the Federalist Papers in support of ratification of the constitution by penning the majority of the essays.[3] Hamilton wrote fifty-one of the eighty-five essays, which are still consulted today by scholars and the Supreme Court.[4] Not only a signer of the constitution, he was one of the main drivers for its ratification in New York, which was vital to the constitution's passage.

Hamilton possessed a skill set that included public speaking, communications, organization, and planning. George Washington recognized this during the Revolutionary War, where Hamilton served as his aide for four years. Later as president, he appointed him as the first Secretary of the Treasury on September 11, 1789.

This suited Hamilton splendidly, as it provided the catalyst for economic planning and introduction of programs that flooded Congress in his first eighteen months in the role, culminating in his report to Congress recommending America's first central bank on December 14, 1790.[5]

Hamilton was acquainted with private banks in Philadelphia, New York, and Boston, but homegrown institutions offered limited guidance in founding a central bank. Fortunately, he was steeped in European banking precedents, for amid the alarums and excursions of the American Revolution he had managed to become educated in financial history. In his astonishingly precocious letter to James Duane of September 1780, the twenty-five-year-old colonel had hit upon an insight that now informed his theory of central banks—the fruitful commingling of public and private money: "The Bank of England unites public authority and faith with private credit. . . . [T]he bank of Amsterdam is on a similar foundation. And why cannot we have an American bank? This hybrid character—an essentially private bank buttressed by public authority—was to define his central bank."[6]

What struck Congress, the president, and all of his contemporaries was the *depth of detail* that Hamilton put into all of his plans. Hamilton was truly a leader with his finger on the pulse of any endeavor or quest he pursued. He went to great lengths to tutor himself on various topics such as banking, where he poured over Malachy Postlethwaite's *Universal Dictionary of Trade and Commerce* and Adam Smith's *Wealth of Nations.*[7]

That is what it takes to master a subject. By diving into the details—*you learn what you didn't know and validate or verify what you thought you knew.* As a result of the exercise you gain real understanding and knowledge based on the experience. We call this *experiential learning,* and the experience is only deepened by participating in the actual work, practices, and procedures of the organization—the *walkabout.*

Hamilton's plan for establishment of the National Treasury and creation of a Central Bank is a great example of implementing vision. He aligned his vision with his mission in a holistic way that not only achieved this goal, which by the way turned out to be incredibly SMART; he addressed the nation's war debt, put the government on sound financial footing, and established commercial banking.[8] Additionally, he was able to convince other nations that the United States was financially sound.[9]

> In 1791, Alexander Hamilton and his Society for Useful Manufactures planned for Paterson, New Jersey to be the center of American industrialism and to reduce the new nation's reliance on foreign industry. Paterson thrived for the next century and a half, and among its manufacturing successes could count the Colt revolver and the first submarine, the latter tested by John Phillip Holland in the Passaic River just above the Great Falls.[10]

This incredible example of holistic planning is what today we look to achieve in our own circumstances as leaders within our own organizations. Achievement is dependent upon effective planning. Not just any plan—*the right plan*—one that is tailored for your particular company or organization. "Planning is bringing the future into the present so that you can do something about it now."[11]

Two types of management that are key in planning are *operational management* and *task management*, and each is made easier through the tools of charts. Each type is critical to the overall success of holistic planning and work in similar yet different ways, as they each gauge different aspects of planning.

The first tool is a flow chart. Flow charts are diagrams that portray the organization's business process activities, information systems, staffing, and other critical aspects that drive and support our mission. They break down our structure in an illustrative way that lets us see the entire organization (holistic picture) all at once, allowing us to process the connections between departments and levels of support. It also provides opportunity to uncover voids, redundancies, and gaps.

Even something as simple and everyday as a bicycle spoke is surrounded by materials, design concepts, and manufacturing processes—leading to solid performance and achievement of getting one down the road to their destination —the goal.

Flow charts provide a look into the core of our operations (*the hub*) for planning and analysis of our operations (*the spokes*) to ensure we are properly structured, staffed (*the bands*), and equipped to carry out our mission (*the rim*) in keeping with the vision. This addresses *operational management* and aids in our strategic planning.

When it comes to *task management*, another vital part of our strategic plan, we look to another useful tool—Gantt charts. They allow us to incorporate expected timelines for each activity into a schedule. Gantt charts allow us to display task dependencies, information flows, and relationships between different activities in any task whether temporary or permanent depending on our mission(s).

This type of chart is common in construction, as it allows all involved, from the management—to the professional—to the contractors, to keep track of progress while appreciating what comes next in the planning, scheduling, and deployment of resources. It is especially helpful in looking at long-lead items to ensure availability and onsite delivery in accordance with the schedule. Nothing brings a project to a screeching halt like a materials delay due to poor planning resulting from unanticipated shortages, work stoppages on the manufacturing end, or delays due to weather, which might include rain, wind, and extreme temperatures.

These are all potential issues that need to be incorporated into the project planning on the front end. Weather events, for instance, are normal and expected occurrences that can be built into the overall project timelines, like snow days in a school calendar—if not needed or used, then students get out early in May or June, depending on what part of the country you are in. In construction it simply means the project will finish early; however, if your delays are based on minor deviations in weather forecasts, such as extended periods of rain, then you have failed to plan properly or the contractor did not make good use of his/her time during good weather days and now you find yourself explaining to stakeholders and accessing liquidated damages (monetary penalties) against the contractor.

In reality boards, stakeholders, and residents understand and can excuse delays or setbacks due to catastrophic events, such as floods, earthquakes, hurricanes, and tornadoes—but trying to blame a major delay on rain, wind, or snow—*not happening*. This expectation and direct accountability permeates all aspects of the organization when it comes to planning.

For those to whom much has been given—*higher salaries, competitive benefits*, and *generous PTO* (paid time off)—much is expected. That is reality-based oversight.

Holistic planning is a multifaceted approach to acquiring the widest possible depth and breadth of information critical to planning in order to align the organization's activities for high-quality outcomes.

Chapter Six

Resource Management
and Its Role in Planning

Putting our thoughts into action in a way that is effective at accomplishing any goal is the very definition of planning. Before we can operationalize any thought we need to develop a plan in a way that is *thoughtful, supported*, and *realistic*. The second of these requirements—*support*—is all about *providing, allocating*, and *employing* resources that are needed in various quantities at various stages of the action(s) of the organization in attainment of goals. This process is called *strategic resource management*, and it plays a central role in accomplishing our plans.

Organizational resources consist of all assets available for use in the production process—*what we make, produce*, or *deliver*—this is why we exist as an organization. This includes physical goods (tangible) and digital goods or services (intangible).

The organization is where resources come together. Organizations use different resources to accomplish goals. The major resources used by organizations are often described as follow: (1) human resources, (2) financial resources, (3) physical resources, and (4) information resources.[1]

An intangible good is a good that does not have a physical nature, as opposed to a physical good (an object). Digital goods, such as downloadable music, mobile apps, or virtual goods used in virtual economies are examples of intangible goods. In an increasingly digitized world, intangible goods play a more and more important role in the economy. Virtually anything that is in a digital form and deliverable on the internet can be considered an intangible good. In the ordinary sense, an intangible good should not be confused with a service since a good is an object, whereas a service is an activity or labor.[2]

The better we are at managing our resources—the longer we will exist and the more profitable or successful we will be. Profit for companies is measured in terms of Gross Profit (Net Sales—Cost of Goods Sold), Operating Profit

(Gross Profit—Operating Costs), and Net Profit (Operating Profit + Any Other Income) – (Additional Expenses) – (Taxes).

Success, however, is measured by a number of factors, including but not limited to achieving mission-critical goals and objectives, especially in non-profits. In schools we look at measuring academic success through indicators and benchmarks that classify us as "high performing." Regardless of the type of organization or business model, neither profit nor success is attainable without strategic management of resources. Without this, we fail, regardless of any amount of planning.

In a service model such as education, a high-performing district means we are turning out students who have mastered the skills necessary to compete on a global scale and gain acceptance into any postsecondary college, university, or trade school in furtherance of their education. Our success is measured through qualitative and quantitative benchmarks that include metrics and rankings such as the following:

- Number of AP (Advanced Placement) courses provided (quantitative) and the percentage of students scoring 4 or better based on scoring set up by The College Board[3] (qualitative in their achievement and quantitative on the number of students scoring over 3).
- ACT scores representing the number of correct answers converted to a score that ranges from 1 to 36 for each of the four tests (English, Mathematics, Reading, and Science) and a composite score that represents the average of those scores.[4]
- SAT scores ranging from 400–1600 based on three components: Evidence-Based Reading and Writing Section: 200–800; Math Section: 200–800; and SAT Essay: Three scores ranging from 2–8.[5]

These benchmarks are utilized along with class rank and other factors to compare and position applicants for acceptance to colleges ranging from "Most Competitive to Less Competitive" developed by Barron's Profiles of American Colleges[6] defined as follows:

BARRON'S MOST COMPETITIVE—"In general, these colleges require high school rank in the top 10 percent to 20 percent and grade averages of A to B+. Median freshman test scores are generally between 655–800 on SAT and above 29 on the ACT. Many of these colleges admit only a small percentage of those who apply—usually lower than one-third."[7]

HIGHLY COMPETITIVE—"Colleges in this group generally look for students with grade averages of B+ to B and accept most of their students from the top 20 percent to 35 percent of the high school class. Median freshman test scores generally range from 620-654 on the SAT and 27 or 28 on the ACT. These schools generally accept between one third and one half of their applicants."[8]

VERY COMPETITIVE—"The colleges in this category generally admit students whose averages are no less that B- and who rank in the top 35 percent to 50 percent of their high school class. Median test scores are in the 573 to 619 range on the SAT and from 24 to 26 on the ACT. These schools generally accept between one half and three quarters of their applicants.[9]

COMPETITIVE—"This category is a broad one covering colleges that generally have median freshman test scores between 500 and 572 on the SAT and between 21 and 23 on the ACT. Some of these colleges require that students have high school averages of B- or better, although some state a minimum of C+ or C. Generally, these colleges prefer students in the top 50 percent to 65 percent of their graduating class and they accept between 75 percent and 85 percent of their applicants."[10]

BARRON'S LESS COMPETITIVE—"Included in this category are colleges with median freshman test scores below 500 on the SAT and below 21 on the ACT. These colleges admit students with averages generally below C who rank in the top 65 percent of their graduating class. These colleges admit 85 percent or more of their applicants.[11]

While these are the current standards for rankings and admission by colleges and universities, there is a growing movement to reduce their impact and importance as benchmarks—led by FairTest, the National Center for Fair and Open Testing.

FairTest, promoting the concept that tests are not everything when predicting future success of students—along with their slogan, "More than a Score"—is gaining ground. While more and more schools are deemphasizing SAT scores as part of the application process and adopting test-optional and test-flexible policies, more than 1,000 accredited colleges and universities have stopped using ACT or SAT scores to admit substantial numbers of students into bachelor degree programs.[12]

Regardless, these test scores are still a leading measure of success in defining high-performance school districts across America. So where does resource allocation come into the discussion? Everywhere, at every stage of student preparation and success. Just like with holistic planning, we need to focus on the whole child as a student to ensure they have *access* and *opportunity* to quality education at every level, pre-kindergarten through grade 12, in order to develop well-rounded students both academically and socially.

The educational services industry is composed of establishments that provide instruction and training on a wide variety of subjects.[13] It is resource intensive, from supplies and materials to delivery of instruction and from curriculum to athletics and fine performing arts. This encompasses highly trained personnel in the form of administration, supervision, teaching, counseling, and a host of support staff.

These institutions, including schools, colleges, universities, and training centers, are either privately or publicly owned. Private institutions may be further classified as "for profit" or "not for profit." We report on publicly traded, for-profit schools that have a focus on postsecondary education. According to the most recent data provided by the US Department of Education, postsecondary education is being provided to about 18.2 million students. Of that population, some 1.4 million are receiving their education through for-profit schools.[14]

The process of attaining the resources necessary to ensure these institutions are successful in achieving their mission begins with budgeting. Budgeting is all about creation of a financial plan in support of the educational road map for districts, universities, or training centers referred to above in the form of an annual operating budget.

In schools the typical budget for acquiring equipment, supplies, and materials represents somewhere between 5 and 10 percent of the budget, and maintaining the necessary staff to support that effort, delivery of instruction, and student support services constitutes roughly 80 percent of the budget. These percentages vary in any given year as the needs change, depending on the district, focus, and direction. Keep in mind we are speaking of the operating budget, not other aspects of budgeting, such as capital projects (Fund 30), which account for major construction projects, or debt service (Fund 40), both of which are in accordance with GAAP (generally accepted accounting principles), a collection of commonly followed accounting rules and standards for financial reporting. Nationwide public schools record and manage these funds in accordance with Statement No. 34 of the Governmental Accounting Standards Board with Fund 30 Capital Projects Fund accounting for major construction and Fund 40 Debt Service to establish and record payments for principal and interest on the bonds issued to finance the construction.[15]

Before we start budgeting in any organization (private or public) we need to know *what we have, what we need,* and *how much those resources are going to cost.* The cost factor is further drilled down into one-time expenses versus recurring costs that will have a direct impact on subsequent budgets, such as lease payments or new positions within the budget.

The main objective in forecasting future budgets is gaining control over current expense needs (expenditures) and funding sources (revenues) to not only consider the current year's impact on taxes in public-funded budgets, reliant on property taxes, or sales revenue in private organizational budgets, but future years as well.

A healthy outlook is three to five years out in order to keep pace with multiyear goals and plans, such as technology, facilities, capital, and staffing and benefits needs. Planning one year at a time is a recipe for disaster; it fails to look ahead and therefore prepare for what is coming down the road.

While there are a host of revenues ranging from state and federal aid, grants, public or private donations, or miscellaneous funds in various types of budgets, the concept is clear—get a handle on what you have now and what you expect in the next year, and plan for what may happen or what you may need in the next three to five years.

That is planning, that is being prepared, that is strategic resource allocation.

In New Jersey, this is made easier, as schools now have the ability to establish and maintain reserve accounts for capital,[16] maintenance, emergency, debt service, and tuition.[17] Deposits into and withdrawals from these reserves allow boards of educations (type II elected) and boards of school estimates (type I appointed) to manage unanticipated budgetary issues or planned improvements (capital projects) that meet the restrictions of each reserve in accordance with the state statutes or administrative code.

The establishment and funding of reserves is crucial in managing cash flow, long-term planning, and avoidance of overdependency of bonding related to construction for any organization whether it be private or public.

For school business officials in New Jersey it is vital given the 2 percent cap on the tax levy increase signed into law by Governor Chris Christie on July 12, 2010.[18] This law made it harder to plan and budget given a prior measure in 2005 revising the calculation of budget caps and reducing allowable surplus for New Jersey public school districts.[19]

Albeit schools operate under the governmental fund structure of GASB, they are very close in structure to private businesses operating under the Financial Accounting Standards Board, or FASB. Both require balance with the difference of "fund equity" compared to "owner's equity":

GASB—Assets = Liabilities + Fund Equity
FASB—Assets = Liabilities + Owner's Equity

Regardless of the accounting standard followed, all organizations and companies must balance their accounts in the form of a trial balance or balance sheet. The balance sheet reports the assets, liabilities, and equity during a specific period. This ensures a company has enough assets, including cash, to balance expenditures. Taking the monetary total of assets (revenues) against the cost of liabilities (expenditures) we see the impact on equity. In business this is accomplished through P&L statements (profit and loss) and net income statements. The goal is first and foremost to be profitable—or we will never be around long enough to capture the vision and accomplish the mission. Another way to describe this is to remain solvent—*able to pay the bills*.

In schools and other nonprofit enterprises, while we may not be looking to profits or calculating net income, we too must concern ourselves with the equity equation by controlling costs—to guard against negative fund balances or reduced equity.

This starts with controlling operational costs (expenditures), which are much different than investments (expenditures), the latter being expenditures designed to acquire program upgrades, new tools, or equipment to benefit the organization or new personnel to enhance our overall competitiveness and gain more return on that investment (ROI). In our example above on schools, with respect to "high-achieving status," those investments could be additional Advanced Placement (AP) course offerings, employment of a college specialist in the high school guidance department, or a one-to-one computer initiative in the form of Chromebooks over various grade levels. These are all investments designed to get us to our ultimate destination on the map—our vision for student achievement and preparation.

Operational expenses are those needed to maintain and support all operations, from salaries, benefits, and insurance to supplies, equipment, and utilities. The larger the operation, the greater the budget; however, cost control measures are what allow us to maximize our available resources and put them into the part(s) of the operation we value most—in education that means into the classroom.

In order to accomplish this, cost control measures need to be systemic, guaranteeing all expenses are properly identified, analyzed, and reviewed for savings without comprising the delivery of services or goods acquired.

We do this all the time in our personal lives, if we live within our own budgets or means, every time we shop by comparing brands and prices to make certain we purchase a quality product at a good if not great price. If quality is not the issue or concern for a temporary or "throw-away" purchase, such as paper plates or cups, we may go with an off brand or generic brand to save our money for another purchase where we won't scrimp.

This can be and is accomplished in high-performing districts and businesses evidenced by their ability to grow, prosper, and expand offerings while maintaining quality programs in school districts and the ability to increase market share for companies in the business world.

As an example, a company or school district can obtain bids or quotes from other vendors that provide the same quality product or service at a better price, which can lower costs. Cost control is an important factor in maintaining and growing profitability or opportunity.

The takeaway—in order to ensure we have the resources needed for allocation to the respective departments or programs in pursuit of our goals, organizations need to remain solvent.

When it comes to budget preparation there are four common types of budgets that companies use: (1) incremental, (2) activity based, (3) value proposition, and (4) zero based.

Let's look at these type of budgets and consider the pros and cons:

1. INCREMENTAL BUDGETING

Incremental budgeting simply applies a percentage or increment to the actual cost in the current year for formulation on next year's budget. This can be a standard percentage applied to items such as supplies or materials and anticipated increases in services based on the CPI (consumer price index) or other market measures, such as inflation, labor rates, or personal consumption expenditures (PCE). Whatever the methodology or index, that percent assumes the status quo and expects year-over-year expenditures will be consistent. If the cost drivers remain consistent it works; however, this type of budgeting fails to take into account changes in the market, new technology, or services and promotes inefficiencies, as some areas of the budget may in fact be overbudgeted to begin with. Thus increasing these budgetary lines just perpetuates the problem, moving the budget amount further from the actual need. Likewise, you can have accounts that are underbudgeted and therefore continue to leave those lines short, requiring constant transfers.

Pros

- Easy to calculate, simple and easy to understand.
- Good for stable budget lines that see little to no change in consumption patterns or price increases such as supplies.

Cons

- Not realistic for large budgets, as it ignores market conditions, such as inflation, which may be lower than the amount used in the calculation.
- It is not sustainable given the constant change in demands on the various line items and problematic with transfers.

- Fails to consider new costs that have no base line or prior years' experience for comparison of budget to actual.
- Lacks fiscal restraint, as there is no incentive to find savings or cut costs based on other needs within the organization that may have a higher priority.

2. ACTIVITY-BASED BUDGETING (ABB)

Activity-based budgeting is designed to allocate spending based according to the activities of the company. It is a system that records, researches, and analyzes activities that lead to costs for a company. Every activity in an organization that incurs a cost is scrutinized for potential ways to create efficiencies.[20]

Pros

- Budget is more in line with organizational targets and ensures a fairer distribution of resources based on actual activity and expense associated with that activity.
- It is more rigorous than incremental budgeting, which merely adjusts the current year for inflation or other indices.
- Activity-based budgeting (ABB) focuses on what is important to the company while instilling fiscal management over expenses, thus reducing costs, generating savings, and allowing for higher retention of profit.
- This method is particularly useful for newer companies and firms undergoing material changes.[21]

Cons

- It is more rigorous than incremental budgeting, which merely adjusts the current year for inflation or other indices.
- Activity-based budgeting (ABB) is more expensive to implement and maintain than traditional budgeting techniques and more time consuming as well.[22]
- Moreover, ABB systems need additional assumptions and insight from management, which can, on occasion, result in potential budgeting inaccuracies.[23]

3. VALUE PROPOSITION BUDGETING (VPB)

A value proposition budget uses financial prioritization based on "value added" for each expenditure in the budget. This is generally not a budget methodology that most businesses follow, as items in any budget should add value or not be in the budget at all. More a mindset than a detailed budgetary process, it focuses on one aspect of budget decision-making, delivering less than effective results. While it has its place in determining value added for expenditures and investments, it is limited if we stick to just this concept.

Pros

- It is more rigorous than incremental budgeting, which merely adjusts the current year for inflation or other indices.
- Product driven—focusing on the value of the product or service produced for the consumer, therefore ensuring quality of product(s) and services.
- Expenditures and investments are considered based on value added, and therefore only items that strengthen or add value to the organization are in the budget.

Cons

- The process is one dimensional with a single purpose, lacking thorough analysis of other factors such as cost containment, spending patterns, or account analysis.
- While important in concept, and an activity that should be part of every budget, it does not exercise enough fiscal discipline to prevent unnecessary expenditures.

4. ZERO-BASED BUDGETING (ZBB)

Zero-based budgeting (ZBB) is a method of budgeting in which all expenses must be justified each year. Prior years' budget allocations are not considered, as the account is reset to zero. The process of zero-based budgeting starts from a "zero base," and every function within an organization is analyzed for its needs and costs.[24]

Budgets are built on a prioritization of need for each budget cycle without concern over prior years' allocations and is, therefore, more reflective of changes in market conditions, such as changes in cost of goods or services needed to continue operations. ZBB allows top-level strategic goals to be implemented into the budgeting process by tying them to specific functional areas of the organization, where costs can be first grouped and then measured against previous results and current expectations.[25] Zero-based budgeting aims to put the onus on managers to justify expenses and to drive value for an organization by optimizing costs and not just revenue.[26]

Pros

- It instills fiscal discipline throughout the budgetary process by requiring justification of all expenditures.
- ZBB promotes awareness of spending patterns and prioritization of actual needs and reduces frivolous spending.
- ZBB starts from zero and calls for a justification of all expenses, including previous allocations as well as recurring expenses in addition to analyzing new expenditures.
- Forces managers to think strategically in prioritizing budget requests that are in line with organizational goals and focus areas.

Cons

- More difficult and time consuming, requiring longer periods of preparation and analysis. Introduces a higher degree of complex financial analysis, ratios, and concepts that some department managers struggle with, therefore requiring more assistance from the operations or accounting division.
- One of the major shortcomings of zero-based budgeting is that it can reward short-term thinking by shifting resources toward areas of companies that will generate revenue over the next calendar year or budgeting period.[27]

In schools there are three typical budget types—program-based budgeting (PBB), site-based budgeting (SBB), or zero-based budgeting (ZBB).

Each has similar *pros* and *cons* to the budget types found in business, with (PBB) closely relating to activity-based budgeting (ABB), as allocations are recorded and prepared based on the programs or activities they support (e.g., nursing, guidance, child study team, library, curriculum development, administration, custodial, maintenance, and transportation) with the bulk of expenditure going to delivery of instruction with salaries, benefits, supplies, and materials.

Site-based budgeting (SBB) involves many of the same principles of PBB; however, it differs in the amount of resources allocated to each school, based on the recognition of different needs at each of those schools. This type of budgeting takes into consideration the changing needs of one location over another in any given budget cycle; however, it creates an opportunity for inequities, depending on how forceful, skillful, or creative one building leader is compared to his/her peers in requesting and supporting the need(s). When left unchecked by central office it can provide the opportunity to create what I refer to as a *"thiefdom."*

As detailed above, ZBB is all about justification of all line items regardless of prior years' allocations or spending, as each new cycle starts at zero. It is also not driven by location or site as with SBB or by program as with PBB, but it too has challenges as presented above. So which is best, optimal, or the one that should be employed?

In reality they all serve good and different purposes designed to acquire resources in furtherance of the organization's mission. Each type of budget addresses different elements of the organization's budgetary actions, including *preparation, implementation, maintenance, monitoring,* and *review*—all components of *strategic resource allocation.*

Regardless of whether the process is employed in a for-profit business, as with private companies, or the business of education with schools—strategic resource allocation promises to get the *right resources* in the *right quantities* delivered to the *right place* at the *right time* at the *best price* to accomplish the *right goals*. For these reasons I suggest a blended approach or combination of these budget types with the goal of optimal operational efficiency (OOE) in a functional model considered *reality-based budgeting* (RBB).

RBB allows us to start with ZBB and to construct our budgets by program PBB to monitor programmatic costs, impacts, and changing needs—as focus areas change over time. At the same time, we need to evaluate different locations of SBB within our organization on a case-by-case basis, as the budget is in progress on a year-to-year basis in planning, as their needs may also warrant additional investment (spending) or reductions (cuts) depending on the review.

By employing each of these budget types in a systemic and systematic way, we ensure optimal results, providing we have a valid plan in this case a budgetary plan that starts with a budget calendar. The purpose of the calendar is to guide all players in the budget process, from managers to executives to stakeholders, in a way that is clearly defined, easy to follow, and comprehensive enough to be both actionable and results oriented.

The budget calendar should include all actions to be taken at each phase of the budget process, from preparation to implementation, by date, action, and responsibility as follows:

- Date—From beginning to end of process
- Action—Detailed description of activities to be completed
- Responsibility—Denoting individual or groups responsible for completion of the action.

Keep in mind resources are limited, and, as such, budgets need to remain flexible, based on ever-present challenges, including but not limited to changes in revenues, reduced or lost funding, and changes in the economy. These challenges have direct impacts on budgets, requiring hard choices in prioritizing when, where, and how those resources are to be deployed, consumed, and transferred within the overall budget and at what cost to the bottom line. Every action is taken at an *opportunity cost* of what else we are forgoing based on those decisions. As managers we must live within our means (available revenue) to balance the budget and remain solvent, referring back to the process of balancing of assets against liabilities to retain equity.

That is reality, and that is why we need to be strategic in managing our resources—that is why we need to develop plans—and why we need to exercise fiscal responsibility in maintaining and implementing those plans.

Chapter Seven

The Financial Benefits of Planning

Recent pop culture has seen Marvel and DC Comics dominating the box office with close to thirty movies in the past decade between the two comic book empires. Marvel's latest *Captain Marvel* (2019) features Carol Danvers, who becomes one of the universe's most powerful heroes when Earth is caught in the middle of a galactic war. Her slogan borrowed from her time in the Air Force is—*Higher, Further, Faster*—which fits nicely into financial goals we set as individuals and organizations.

Think about it . . . through *proper planning* we can ensure our goals of: attaining greater success (*higher*); enjoying long-term success (*further*), and meeting those goals quicker (*faster*).

Successful planning allows us to benefit in many ways—chiefly growing our companies financially through profitability and development of reserves for future needs and building our reputation as solid performers in a sea of competition. Again we continue to be measured by key performance indicators (KPIs) and satisfaction levels of those we serve—our stakeholders and customer base—which keeps us accountable.

Irrespective of the type of organization you are a part of, everyone wants to achieve great things over a long period of time. Otherwise, we fall victim to the "flash in the pan" or "one-hit-wonder" category, only to find ourselves confronting one setback after another, until we lose the very groups we are striving to satisfy. That's how organizations who were once successful and dominant in their respective fields or markets fall into the abysmal realm of failed companies.

With institutions that must continue, such as public education institutions (schools), while they may not go out of business, they are subject to state takeovers and loss of financial aid depending on the level of decline and mismanagement often tied to poor student achievement and or poor financial performance. The latter is often related to the former in situations where the first poor decision is simply "throwing money at the problem," a topic I will address in detail in the next book of the series on problem-solving.

The financial benefits of planning are derived from embarking on a disciplined journey, one in which your path is clearly defined and your mission is known to all who travel with you. It means we have purpose, direction, understanding, and the resources necessary to go the distance. Once again, it is all tied back to strategic planning and allocation of resources.

Strategy is what allows our plans to achieve major outcomes and accomplish our overall aim. It is the difference maker between failure or mediocre results versus success and attainment of our goals. "With a strong strategic plan; organizations can be proactive rather than merely reacting to situations as they arise. Being proactive allows organizations to keep up with the ever-changing trends in the market and always stay one step ahead of the competition."[1]

In a competitive world, planning is what gives us the advantage over others who fail to plan; in business that means succeeding where others fail; in schools that means delivering on promises to stakeholders by achieving our mission—to provide students with a superior educational experience.

Fiscal responsibility is what allows us to generate, maintain, and deploy financial resources necessary to equip our teams, departments, and organizations with the ability to plan. Without funding—there is no plan. That is about as real as it gets. Money may not drive every decision in business, and it is not always the first consideration in goal attainment; however, absent money (drafts, money orders, notes, bonds, capital, fund balance, funding) you have no business. That is why we need to plan financially for the success of businesses and organizations to ensure long-term survival and allow those businesses and organizations to fulfill their missions. Financial planning provides advantages to help us achieve that task.

FOUR ADVANTAGES OF FINANCIAL PLANNING FOR ORGANIZATIONS

1. *Generation of Fund Balances*—Building or improving account balances is a deliberative process achieved through awareness, action, and focus.
2. *Improved Budgetary Discipline*—Our budgets become better and more disciplined focusing on what we need and what is vital to our success.

3. *Strengthening of Bond Ratings*—Financial planning instills fiscal discipline that allows organizations to pay off debt and move to a "pay-as-you-go" structure for capital needs.
4. *Allowance for Developmental Planning*—With healthy balances and lower operational costs, organizations can start planning for the goals and initiatives with more available resources.

Whenever we focus on anything . . . we get better at it; budgeting and fiscal management are no exception. When we add the element of *discipline* to our *planning* we achieve better results regardless of what we are planning—this includes *financial planning*.

Discipline concentrates our focus into laser-like precision. It refines our approach and converts it into progress, motivation, and ultimate achievement. Take, for instance, weight loss and fitness. When we focus on a fitness plan that includes physical training, workouts, and healthy choices in our diets, we see quicker and better results that are sustainable for longer periods than dieting alone or simply working out.

Think about energy conservation or any other targeted approach to savings—once we make a concerted effort to improve energy management practices, such as turning off the lights, replacing bulbs with energy efficient ones, and including energy ratings into the purchases of appliances, we see an immediate reduction in our energy bills. The initial improvement or drop is huge, much like weight loss when we start to work out. However, the initial gains, or in this case losses, are soon reversed as the attention and focus wains. Months later we are back on the scale and looking at higher energy bills, as all the lights in the house are on while running multiple devices. Without discipline we achieve short-term gains that begin to diminish and fade over time.

Let's look at another area of operations that has a major impact on finances and debt issuance—facilities construction. Construction in any business is driven by new construction (expansion) or rehabilitation (remodeling), depending on the needs, which in turn define the scope and budget.

Estimating the cost of any project with absolute precision is impossible due to a number of variables, such as materials available and selected, unforeseen conditions requiring contingencies, and changes in market conditions, like labor rates based on supply and demand. For this reason, we need to rely on skilled estimators to account for these factors when creating an accurate estimate. The accuracy of a cost estimate relies on a number of things: the quality of the project plan; the level to which the estimator defines a project; the experience and skill of the estimator; the accuracy of cost information; and the quality of any tools and procedures the estimator uses.[2] In many cases project costs are estimated by a dollar per square foot of construction that varies depending on new or rehabilitation and market conditions (labor, materials and inflation). These costs can grow significantly over time, as prices go up roughly 3 percent per year, as long as the construction industry is booming and the market forces of supply and demand favor the contractors. "When construction is very actively growing, total construction costs typically increase more rapidly than the net cost of labor and materials. In active markets overhead and profit margins increase in response to increased demand."[3]

Construction is a major contributor to the US economy. The industry has more than 680,000 employers with over seven million employees and creates nearly $1.3 trillion worth of structures each year.[4] Construction spending averaged $1.3 trillion per month at a seasonally adjusted annual rate from April 2019 through August 2019, according to estimates from the US Census Bureau released under their table of values for construction with a slight decrease of 1.9 percent from August of 2018.[5] However while total construction (private and public) was down slightly for this period, public construction rose 4.6 percent with commercial construction up 23.6 percent over the previous period (August 2018). That represents significant growth, driving construction prices up significantly, resulting in higher bids.

So what does this mean to us as managers over this segment of organizational operations related to planning?

It means we need to be prepared to plan better in preparation of project specifications and determination of design solutions that address the needs of our facilities both existing (renovations) and planned (new) to avoid unnecessary cost overruns and change orders prior to going out to bid, awarding projects, and breaking ground. The best plans and best practices involve assembling the right team of professionals (architects, engineers, and construction managers) to maximize cost savings while achieving quality projects. Again this starts with planning.

Michael Wozny, director of Educational Projects at EI Associates, a leading architectural and engineering firm with offices in Cedar Knolls, New Jersey; Harrisburg, Pennsylvania; and Newark, Delaware, refers to it as the Maximum Value Curve (MVC).

As an educational facilities planner he promotes the concept of larger savings in the planning phase for any project(s), noting the larger the project, the more opportunity to save up front through better planning during the initial planning phase. This allows any organization to maximize those savings by evoking the same planning concepts addressed in other aspects of the operation to find their way into construction and remediation of site and building projects, from roofs to boiler or window to doors.

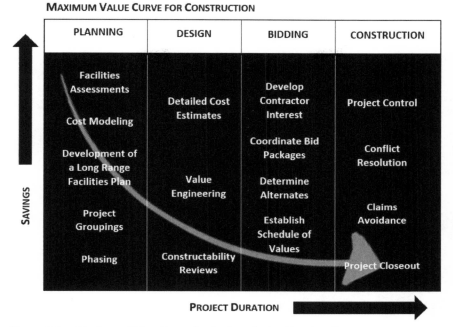

MAXIMUM VALUE CURVE FOR CONSTRUCTION

PLANNING	DESIGN	BIDDING	CONSTRUCTION
Facilities Assessments		Develop Contractor Interest	Project Control
Cost Modeling	Detailed Cost Estimates		
Development of a Long Range Facilities Plan	Value Engineering	Coordinate Bid Packages	Conflict Resolution
		Determine Alternates	
Project Groupings		Establish Schedule of Values	Claims Avoidance
Phasing	Constructability Reviews		Project Closeout

SAVINGS

PROJECT DURATION

Figure 7.1. Maximum Value Curve for Savings during Construction

As presented in figure 7.1 the three phases (planning, design, and bidding) offer the real opportunity to save with planning resulting in the largest impact on savings. By the time we are in construction you are playing defense with conflict resolution and claims avoidance as compared with value engineering an offensive play prior to breaking ground.

When undertaking larger projects, such as designing new buildings or adding additions to schools, hospitals, or other facilities that expand through growth, the potential for savings is huge. The premise is simple and in line with the concept of this book, "stirred in the front"—the time to address any complex issue is in the planning phase.

Our catchphrase of *higher, further, faster* lends itself once more to the financial benefits of construction planning the same way as any other aspect of our operations with the goal being to achieve quality projects. Quality projects that exceed expectations (higher)—extend the life of our facilities (further)—and are completed on time (faster). The ultimate goal with any construction is to finish on time and underbudget and deliver a quality project, the measure of any successful project.

In order to go *higher*, *further*, and *faster* we need fuel, and in businesses that means money, whether it is funding derived from sales revenue, grants, taxes, or bank loans. Without it, we are not going anywhere quick; instead it is more like *lower*, *slower*, and *shorter*.

That is why financial planning is so important. A strategic plan of this type focuses not only on budgeting for expenditures (fixed and nonfixed costs) but also concentrates on revenues to support the plans we create. This requires strong fiscal oversight in establishing and monitoring specific and measurable financial goals that are part of the overall strategic plan for the organization. Once the financial plan is complete—it is the responsibility of all managers within the organization to take ownership in operationalizing the plan on a coordinated and integrated basis, thus enabling the organization to operate efficiently and effectively.

FOUR BENEFITS OF FINANCIAL PLANNING FOR ORGANIZATIONS

Positive Cash Flow

Cash flow is the net amount of cash and cash equivalents available for reallocation through transfers or set aside for future investments. It is a measure of financial solvency of the company and shows how effective the used financial resources are to generate additional cash for future investments.[6] Generation of positive cash flow should be a goal when anticipating end-of-year targeted purchasing (purchasing plan) or substantial capital expenditures in the near future or for existing project needs that are outside of the budget. This allows the needed flexibility for items that had been previously identified as a legitimate need; however, they were not high enough on the priority list to make the budget. This is especially helpful with facility-related expenditures that would further burden future budgets.

Asset Management

Financial planning provides the framework for asset acquisition, recording, allocation, and disposition. Disposition of property, plant, and equipment refers to the disposal of the company's assets. This can include the sale, exchange, abandonment, and involuntary termination of the asset's service.[7] Asset management provides the controls to ensure we know: what we have, what we need, and how much we need and where it is. As part of our overall risk management it serves as safeguard against theft. It also protects against overordering or stockpiling and plans out purchases to stagger larger capital needs, such as vehicle fleets or equipment that should be on replacement cycles to avoid mass replacement in any given year, which in turn drains resources and impacts cash flow in a negative manner.

Accelerate Savings

While cash flow helps to generate available funds that can sweep to surplus in any given period (monthly, quarterly, or annually), a dedicated savings goal in any financial plan allows those savings to be realized quicker with greater balances. This is true in establishing reserves or fund balances, as companies and organizations face monetary decisions related to disposition of profits or surpluses.

When a savings or fund-generation plan is in place, it allows for the deposit of those funds to reach the predetermined targets and accomplishment of the goal. In some instances, the target amounts may require a multiyear plan or commitment; however, again we are given the means to track our progress through financial reporting along with visuals (graphs and charts) that provide the opportunity to reaffirm our commitment and capture our progress, thus keeping us on track and focused to go the distance.

Confidence

Nothing instills confidence or builds trust faster than operating under the guise of a well-crafted and defined plan. Financial plans help promote this concept as they demonstrate accountability, foresight, discipline, and control. This is especially critical when dealing with money, as gaining financial trust becomes harder and requires more work.

People have a propensity to apply a skeptical degree of caution when it comes to trusting organizations and finances given the recent history of abuse of that trust with individuals like Bernie Madoff, who confessed to a $65 billion Ponzi scheme.[8] Add to this some high-profile corporate cases, Enron, WorldCom, and Fannie Mae, and we see the need for transparency, independent review, and changes in reporting requirements.

So the real challenge in gaining and maintaining that trust is reconciling the concern of fraud or theft with the willingness to trust and gain confidence in the overall financial operations of any business or organization. This is achieved through communications of the plan to capture this benefit.

Communicating the financial plan through messaging opportunities allows organizations to promote the plan and in turn monitor its health and success—back to awareness. Opportunities such as public meetings or stakeholder events allow for presentations, updates, or reports depending on the forum. Formal reporting throughout the year with a comprehensive annual financial report (CAFR), containing the management discussion and analysis (MD&A) section, and an annual report help to ensure integrity of the financial plan and financial reporting on a regular basis with monthly, quarterly, and annual statements that are independently reviewed and validated bolster that confidence.

While the strategic plan remains the engine that powers the vision—it is the financial plan that fuels our progress and therefore remains critical in supporting the drive in obtaining our goals. Therefore, we must ensure we are running on a full tank at the outset and keep refilling the tank as those revenues are depleted from operating expenses and investments. This requires a financial plan that is capable of providing both the advantages and benefits that allow for our success at the *speed of trust*.[9]

Chapter Eight

Goal Attainment

Goal attainment or success is reached when our actual results match our desired outcomes. This is when we celebrate and look back over the road to success to understand and capture *what worked* to make it part of our *best practices* for future goal attainment and rule out *what did not*—the actions or *pitfalls* that delayed our progress—to make certain we do not repeat them. This is part of what the military refers to as the *debrief*—examining the overall process to improve future outcomes.

Debriefing is a simple skill that represents one of the most significant lessons learned in recent decades: organizations that fail to continuously revise their assumptions about their operating environment (i.e., market) will soon face obsolescence or irrelevance. A swiftly changing market can render limited professional skill sets obsolete almost overnight. Organizations must develop the capacity to learn from a changing environment by creating a formal learning structure that fosters agility and preserves knowledge.[1]

In February 2017 in Miami, Florida, I enjoyed a lengthy conversation with Matt "Hobo" Brady of AfterBurner, Inc., a consulting group of prior military fighter pilots. We shared our personal experiences of leading successful teams in the military during our respective tours of duty. This lead to an article that appeared in the April 2019 edition of *School Business Affairs*.[2]

While our enlistments were decades apart, the strategies, concepts, and elements of planning remained the same, including debriefing after every mission. Whether you're flying an $18.8 million F16, managing teams processing TOP SECRET—FLASH message traffic in a maximum security facility (SCIF), or managing the strategic plan of an organization, debriefing after every campaign, project, or major initiative is a critical step in the process of improving future outcomes.

Debriefing provides a powerful and essential structure for maintaining the capacity to learn. When we create lessons learned through the debriefing process, we are generating a form of knowledge called explicit knowledge. In knowledge management theory, there are two types of knowledge—explicit and tacit. Explicit knowledge is simply knowledge that can be written down and/or stored. Tacit knowledge, however, is complex and difficult to codify and, therefore, resides only in the minds of human beings. Tacit knowledge is closely related to the concepts of skill and experience.[3]

Debriefing should become part of every mission regardless of how long or in-depth the mission is; however, longer, complicated missions may require longer periods and multiple meetings to ascertain all of the critical performance pieces of those missions, which leads to our next point—some missions take longer to plan, stage, initiate, and execute. We have often heard the adage, "Anything worth doing takes time." When it comes to big ideas and big payoffs, organizational missions can take place over multiple years, budgets, and changing personnel, including leadership.

Success is not easy and it's never quick—it comes at a price, and that price is not always in terms of monetary costs, like start-up capital or investment spending. It requires personal sacrifice in terms of time, energy, stress, and commitment. This means rolling up our sleeves and getting in there to do what needs to be done—day in and day out—and staying the course to see it through to completion; we are talking about "nose to the grindstone" level commitment—hard work. There are no shortcuts. "That is the only way to get what we want in the real world, we won't get anything by wishing for it or just wanting it, a price is demanded and a price must be paid."[4]

This sage advice was underscored in the 1987 movie *Wall Street* where Lou Mannheim played by Hal Holbrook pulls a young, eager, and misguided stockbroker Bud Fox (Charlie Sheen) aside to remind him, "There are no shortcuts. Quick-buck artists come and go with every bull market, but the steady players make it through the bear markets."[5] This advice goes unheeded as Fox leaves Jackson Steinem in handcuffs, crying. The film closes out with young Bud on the steps of the federal court building facing charges of insider trading and market manipulation.

While shortcuts are not necessarily related to felony charges or linked to un-ethical practices, the premise here is one must follow the plan and do the leg-work necessary to secure the lasting success as it builds stronger foundations.

The bigger the goal, the higher the price—that is the unspoken rule that has been floating around for thousands of years. Shortcuts have been and can be taken, but shortcuts will rarely lead you to permanent success. Short-cuts will not make you an extraordinary individual; they will not make you exceptional. Sometimes, it is actually not what you achieve but what you become along the way and who you help along the way that makes it so rich and rewarding.[6]

Shortcuts or cutting corners leaves us vulnerable to outside criticism when plans go off course and internal unrest when those on the front lines are ignored when pointing out measures that must be taken or guidelines that must be followed to prevent such deviations.

This level of commitment needs to extend to our entire staff, managers, and team leaders who are vital to the plan's success and as such need to maintain the same level of dedication that requires long hours, tough decision-making, and loyalty. Loyalty is what extends the effort through the tough times when the end goal seems far from sight and it is easier to quit. This is where leadership plays a key role in *maintenance of effort* to stay on course. It is easy to celebrate the success; however, without this type of leadership and dedication we will never get to the finish line.

Acknowledging difficulties is not a sign of giving up or giving in; it demonstrates your grasp on reality—not only on the issues and what's at stake but your understanding of those in the trenches and on the front lines and what they're up against. The struggle is real, but in the renowned words of Frederick Douglass, "If there is no struggle, there is no progress"—that is reality.

Bertie Charles Forbes, better known as B.C. Forbes, a Scottish-born American financial journalist, author, and founder of *Forbes* magazine, believed this—as he put it in his words, "A price has to be paid for success. Almost invariably those who have reached the summits worked harder and longer, studied and planned more assiduously, practiced more self-denial, overcame more difficulties than those of us who have not risen so far."[7]

Life always gets harder as you approach the summit.—Random Fortune Cookie

A smart and accomplished colleague once told me in her house they have a saying, *"Success is never owned, it is rented . . . and the rent comes due every day!"*—Thanks, Deb.

We meet people throughout our lives that influence the way we think, act, and view situations, our work, and the way we approach leadership. I always gravitate to those who are optimistic, hardworking, insightful, and motivated. These are the people we enjoy, draw inspiration from, and learn from. They are almost always successful. *These are people we want running our companies or serving in key leadership roles*, as their enthusiastic spirit and positive attitude becomes infectious in inspiring those around them to do more than they thought was possible.

At the same time, we shouldn't look to avoid pessimistic people, but instead work to turn them more positive by focusing on good things or things they like about the organization or process. While it is not always easy, it is necessary as they are part of the team.

These are individuals who center on negativity, view challenges as problems, and avoid seeking solutions. Some waste more energy on complaining and what I call *problem addiction*—going negative regardless of the number of solutions provided to them.

This attitude or practice of accepting a situation as it "is" and living with it is tantamount to giving up or going hopelessly into the fray. These are people without vision. *These are not the people we want running our companies or leading our teams.*

However, with strong support and resources available, such as employee assistance programs (EAPs), counseling and mental health clinicians (if needed), or simply just helping them to experience a positive outlook, they can become productive. They now have a chance to improve their personal situation(s) and become productive individuals, who in turn can become positive leaders who make positive contributions in our organizations. Regardless of the level of leadership they reach, they become happier individuals and, as a result, happier employees.

This is perhaps the fastest-growing issue in schools, companies, and organizations today, as more individuals are experiencing social and emotional issues that interfere with their ability to focus, learn, and achieve. That is why EAPs are necessary to provide support that our employees may need that is beyond our scope to prevent, diagnose, and treat.

> Employee assistance programs (EAPs) provide a range of different services and resources. In general, EAPs provide assessment and services for addressing a range of personal problems and concerns that interfere with employees' well-being and work performance (EASNA, 2009). EAPs may help individuals with emotional and substance use issues, interpersonal relationships, legal problems, and financial difficulties. In addition, EAPs may provide information and resources on health promotion and work/life issues. EAP professionals may also provide training and/or consultation to managers and supervisors on organizational concerns. Furthermore, EAPs may be helpful to employees experiencing serious illness and the associated challenges of staying at work or returning to work. (National Business Group on Health, 2013)[8]

By recognizing and supporting this need, we are providing that chance to make positive improvements in their lives, which has a direct impact on their attitude and performance in work.

The reality is negative or pessimistic individuals exist for a differing reasons. They are all around us. We find them in our personal lives, organizations, and even on our teams. We need to work to make experiences better for them by instilling positive thoughts, actions, and reflections on our mission, the vision, and what it means for them. All the while working to cultivate a positive influence on the environment and culture—one that sticks—one that stays positive. In fact, we need to do our best to transform their negativity into positive energy that benefits them, the team, and the organization.

As managers we need to be great leaders, we need to inspire others to do more, reach higher, and accomplish any and every mission. This means we need all involved in the process, and as such we want to avoid high turn-over or terminations. This starts by protecting our investment in personnel by growing their skill, knowledge, and experience to increase productivity and gain greater value; however, there are times when separation is not only necessary but the best thing to do for survival of the mission and the organi-zation. While this should be the last resort, we sometimes find it is the only option to maintain positive momentum to remain engaged in pursuit of our goals—keeping us on track as a unit.

Positive people are resilient—they bounce back and refuse to give up. Growing up we called it "grit"—courage, resolve, or strength of character. Today, it is resurfacing in leadership conversations and studies noting its presence in individuals who are successful despite challenges and setbacks they have experienced. The *Wall Street Journal* ran with it in an op-ed piece titled, "Is There Anything Grit Can't Do?"[9] The *New York Times* discussed it in their article, "Putting Grit in Its Place,"[10] referring to the book *Grit: The Power of Passion and Perseverance*, a number-one *New York Times* best-seller by Angela Duckworth, professor of psychology at the University of Pennsylvania and the founder and CEO of Character Lab. The article points out how Duckworth notes, "That the quality of our longing matters. Gritty people are resilient and hardworking, sure. But they also know, in a very, very deep way what it is they want."[11]

Knowing what you want is easy—getting what you want requires work.

I was once asked to describe myself in one word—without hesitation I re-sponded, "Driven." Grit is a characteristic trait found in individuals who are driven. People who are driven have a determination that knows no quit. In the words of Hannibal, "Aut inveniam viam aut faciam"—"I shall either find a way or make one."[12] This is often the difference between success and failure, as we all experience setbacks from time to time on the way to achieving our goals. Those who quit or give up will never make it to the desired goal, and some just stay frozen in the moment of what could have been while listing the reasons why they did not make it so.

True Grit,[13] in the style of John Wayne playing Marshall Rooster Cogburn in the 1969 American Western film, had one other quality that made the *grit* real—*attitude*. That same *attitude* resurfaced on the big screen in 2010 during the second adaptation,[14] with executive producer Stephen Spielberg and staring Jeff Bridges as Cogburn.

What the films have in common besides characters and plot is both rely on a mix of attitude and grit to achieve success. While separate in meaning, together they are inseparable. They feed each other with an emotional adrenaline in a way that provides a super boost to our efforts. In presentations or keynotes I explain the relationship between success and attitude this way:

The difference in success and failure is not based on effort, anyone can try . . . it's attitude . . . a determination to succeed regardless of the obstacles before you. This requires grit.

So back to positive people who emanate hope, vision, and success. I recently had the privilege of meeting Dennis Budinich, senior vice president and chief culture officer of Investors Bank, headquartered in Short Hills, New Jersey. With regional banks throughout New Jersey and New York, over ninety-three years of corporate history and $25 billion in assets, Investors has grown into one of the largest banks headquartered in New Jersey.

Dennis was tapped as the first culture officer in the banking industry by chairman and CEO Kevin Cummings not simply because of his credentials, which are impressive, but because of his outlook on life, culture, and value in people. Dennis is one of those guys who plans for the future by living it every day with the goal in mind of what we all can achieve to make things better for ourselves, our teams, our businesses, and our organizations.

He is the perfect person to share the mission and vision that Investors is built on with a foundation of four core values: cooperation, character, community, and commitment.

It is as evident for them as an organization today, as it was the day I met Kevin in 2009, when he first shared them with me in his office after winning a banking RFP with our district. Going over the *transition plan* to ensure a smooth changeover, I knew it was going to be a successful partnership with individuals who matched our own vision and expectations. What impressed me then and continues to impress me years later is how genuine, direct, and open Kevin and his team are about attaining their goals to achieve success. Their path includes hard work, determination, superior service, and a sense of community that extends beyond a slogan or tagline. They work to become interwoven into the fabric of the communities they serve, evidenced by the "weave logo" becoming not only a solid business partner but a trusted neighbor as well. As a result, they have enjoyed incredible success as an organization trading on NASDAQ at a share price of $12.58 (October 24, 2019),[15] up 218 percent from $3.95 per share on October 5, 2005, fourteen years ago.

Their website confirms that commitment to community as visitors to the site find a Community tab right on the banner of the main page. With one click, you have access to "The Weave," their blog, written by Investors Bank employees. Employees—not top management. That means empowering employees to share their thoughts, strategies, and value added to the organization they are a part of—showcasing their talents, drive, and esprit de corps, what *Webster's* describes as "The common spirit existing in the members of a group and inspiring enthusiasm, devotion, and strong regard for the honor of the group."[16] That is living by your word—that is putting your values into action—that is what earns your success.

One strong indicator of their success is the high retention rate of key leaders within the organization. The same individuals who onboarded us in 2009 are still with the organization in 2019.

The four pillars or core values for Investors Bank are defined as follows:

Cooperation: The act of working together toward a common purpose or benefit

Character: The combination of features and traits that form the individual nature of a person or team

Community: A self-organized network of people who collaborate by sharing ideas and information for the sake of the common good

Commitment: A pledge, promise, or obligation

Dennis talks about fundamental steps in making positive change in any organizational culture by changing the mindset of those who come to work through four words: *hope, optimism, purpose,* and *happiness.*

When we as leaders create, foster, and maintain positive environments that are supportive, encouraging, and exciting, our people will grow, learn, and excel.

When individuals are happy, they have hope; when they have purpose, they have meaning; and when they are optimistic, they are operating under an attitude of "can-do." Just because we are challenged does not mean we have to lose any of these four important tenets of positive culture.

There will be struggle, there will be pain, there will be sacrifice, but as discussed in the opening of this chapter, we will overcome as individuals, teams, and organizations. With each battle, each tussle, each skirmish, we become tested and hardened like steel. As teams, these are the experiences that bond us to each other and to the organizations we serve. Going through a tough period and coming out on top provides a unique experience, not only shared but something that now belongs to us and we belong to it—that is our *shared experience.*

Chapter Nine

Contingency Planning

"What If?"

Real planning begins when we look beyond the probable and start to consider the possible, regardless of how remote it may be; even if there is a chance that it can happen, we need to plan for it. Most of the people who say "that's impossible" are left dazed and confused when the impossible becomes reality. They are taken aback and oftentimes defeated not because they are incapable of action or simply stand by while the drama unfolds. It is because they now lack the most valuable resource in planning—time.

Time allows us to prepare, to consider, to query—all the while testing our hypotheses and gathering facts to validate or contradict our means and methods to ensure success in the long run.

This is *when* and *where* we need to ponder the *what if* scenarios and look for ways to avoid defeat by arming our plan with countermeasures.

I remember a few years ago a board member saying this to me as we were finishing the final stages of our annual budgeting plan and preparing for the public presentation. I informed him that "what if" scenarios were part of our budgetary planning. He was pleased to hear, as he regularly incorporated this element of planning in his own business.

For us it started years earlier when the governor at the time, Chris Christie, had pulled all our state aid one week before we were set to present the budget for final approval in 2010. Districts across New Jersey were left scrambling to figure out how to cut, reduce, and eliminate programs to meet a budgetary shortfall that no one saw coming—talk about the impossible.

One week prior we had the commissioner of education, Bret Schundler, on our middle school stage in Summit, New Jersey, during a state meeting to address school funding amid a troubled state budget with revenue shortfalls due to a state pension crisis, among other challenges. The commissioner stated that districts across the state were looking at around 3 to 5 percent reductions—with the worst-case scenario at 15 percent. Six days later we lost 100 percent, or $2.6 million.

Were we able to make the cuts and reduce the budget based on the total loss of state aid? Yes, but what we learned was *lack of time made the task painfully difficult*. What we did moving forward was to integrate "what if" scenarios, like losing state aid, into our planning each year.

The business of education like any industry has its own challenges and influences such as state and federal funding, legislative initiatives, unfunded mandates, and competition from private and charter schools along with growing pressure from choice schools and specialized academies. Keep in mind we must answer to the parents, the governing body, the taxpayers, the community, and the state and federal governments—our audience market.

Let's look at another industry that we are all familiar with, retail, in particular, department stores and the consumer cyclical sector of diversified media.

In retail, successful plans take into consideration changes in the economy, changes in customer purchasing, and changes in technology, all of which have transformed the retail markets into home shopping bonanzas. With Amazon and your cell phone you can view, select, order, and pay without leaving the couch. Best of all, the goods arrive within days, or if you upgrade to Prime—next day. If you think it's not a big deal, take a trip to your local mall.

Not too long ago my wife asked the question we all struggle with, "What do you feel like for dinner tonight?" I jumped up and said let's go to California Pizza Kitchen, so off we went to the one in our area at Willowbrook Mall in Wayne, New Jersey.

We hadn't been to the mall in a while; I used to live at that mall when I was in high school. It was always packed and you ran into everyone you knew because if you wanted it you had to get it at the mall.

The mall is not so crowded anymore, like malls across the country, and we rarely see anyone we know, not even those working in the stores. It used to be such a part of our lives. We parked next to Sears and walked on the outside to the restaurant entrance. After dinner, I said let's go through the mall and go out through Sears; I wanted to see what they did with it, as it was recently cut in half based on the slump in sales. A couple of years ago they subdivided the back half and eliminated the outdoor area to allow a new Dave & Buster's, a family-friendly chain offering a sports-bar-style setting for American food and arcade games.

As we walked and talked about the old stores that are gone like Radio Shack, Sam Goody, and KB Toys, we entered the Sears, only to see store closing signs stating, "Everything Must Go!"

Walking though Sears it was unbelievable to see what had become of the once anchor store in the mall. We were witnessing the end of an era brought about by failure to plan for the evolution of online buying.

Remember Borders? What about Circuit City, Tower Records, or Musicland? Those stores were all big chains back in 1995, when Amazon debuted. But now they're all gone, due in part to the online retailer upending the American retail landscape.

Jeff Bezos's company has been blamed for killing off once-stalwart retail chains. To hear some tell it, the path to total Amazon domination is just beginning. One investment firm even has a "Death by Amazon" index to track the stock prices of 54 retail chains they believe are most threatened by the online retailer.[1]

This kind of impact and upheaval forces companies that are considered impenetrable to fall in an unexpected or sound defeat. In true David-and-Goliath fashion, Amazon had brought down a company—twenty years ago you wouldn't think it was possible.

"Of course, Amazon isn't solely responsible for killing struggling stores. Bad leadership and strategic mistakes have crippled companies like Sears and JCPenney just as much, according to some."[2]

As presented in chapter 3, planning is all about orientation, knowing where you are, and knowing where you want to be and then laying out a course to get there in the quickest time while avoiding the most amount of obstacles.

A close friend of mine once said, "In life, there is no reverse . . . only forward." The phrase was born out of a harrowing sailboat experience with his adult daughter off the cost of St. Martins in which they were given a faulty monohull whose propeller was not properly attached. If they went into reverse the propeller would work its way loose and fall off. The ship mechanic who came out to assist them hollered out as he was leaving, "Remember, there is no reverse . . . only forward." This later became a trademark of the trip, as his daughter got him a shirt with the words embroidered, *Life, there is no reverse . . . only forward.* Like any good story we laughed, and we're entertained, but the words stuck with me. It made the point that planning is all about moving forward . . . like life. We do not get many do-overs nor do we have the ability to put it into reverse. We must continue to move forward and deal with what comes our way.

Like the story about Sears, other retailers like JCPenney and more share the fate of failing to plan for the changing market conditions that gave or give rise to Amazon and other online upstarts like Zappos for their creativity and ability to seize an opportunity that many had doubted when they began.

Recognizing the direct threat from Amazon, Macy's has enacted counter-measures as part of their plan to ward off a similar fate by devising a plan that includes: mobile checkout at some stores with plans to introduce it to 450–650 locations, introduction of a pilot program to offer virtual reality furniture shopping experiences, and focusing on private labels such as Michael Kors.

"Arguably, no retailer has more to lose from the rise of Amazon (NASDAQ:AMZN) than Macy's (NYSE:M). The venerable department store chain was a giant of retail throughout the 20th century, with flagship stores in many of the country's biggest cities, but the rise of e-commerce has threatened Macy's like nothing before it."[3]

The concept of buying online was once considered a bit of a joke, as we needed to touch and try out or try on the merchandise. Amazon worked that out as well, with liberal return policies and easy prepackaging that includes prepaid shipping labels, thus eliminating the risk. As a result, sales soared. Amazon posted revenues of $232.9 billion in 2018 with a gross profit of $93.7 billion. Planning and execution drove the stock from $1.50 per share in May 1997 to an all-time high of $2,012.71 in September 2018 and now sits at $1,761.83 as of August 2019.[4]

Buying online in 1997 was as about as trusted as buying products made in Japan in 1967. Today, both have become reality and trusted. Digital natives have no fear associated with buying online or online payment services. The boomers are starting to catch on once they discover the ease at which the process really happens. The world is changing and change will never stop. We must embrace it and plan for it, or we too will be left behind.

Amazon innovated what Sears created in their original business model—the Sears & Roebuck Catalog.

Richard Warren Sears started a business selling watches through mail order catalogs in Redwood Falls, Minnesota in 1888. By 1894, the Sears catalog had grown to 322 pages, featuring sewing machines, bicycles, sporting goods, automobiles (produced from 1905–1915 by Lincoln Motor Car Works of Chicago, not related to the current Ford Motor Company brand of the same name) and a host of other new items.

Organizing the company so it could handle orders on an economical and efficient basis, Chicago clothing manufacturer Julius Rosenwald became a part-owner in 1895. By the following year, dolls, refrigerators, stoves and groceries had been added to the catalog. Sears, Roebuck and Co. soon developed a reputation for high quality products and customer satisfaction. By 1895, the company was producing a 532-page catalog with the largest variety of items that anybody at the time could have imagined. "In 1893, the sales topped 400,000 dollars. Two years later they exceeded 750,000 dollars."

In 1906 Sears opened its catalog plant and the Sears Merchandise Building Tower. And by that time, the Sears catalog had become known in the industry as "the Consumers' Bible." In 1933, Sears, Roebuck and Co. produced the first of its famous Christmas catalogs known as the "Sears Wishbook," a catalog featuring toys and gifts and separate from the annual Christmas Catalog.[5]

Amazon "e-order" capitalized on use of both UPS (United Parcel Service) and USPS (United States Postal Service). However, their latest progression is to take over the delivery with their own fleet of trucks or use of Amazon Prime Lockers at remote locations. This online giant has also partnered with Kohls for returns, which was also smart on the part of Kohls to maintain and increase foot traffic. Amazon's constant planning includes looking into drones as part of the logistics for delivering goods to homes.

Walmart is a brick-and-mortar retailer that is branching out to maintain market share and maintain relevance with offers such as online purchasing, next-day shipping, and online grocery ordering with express lane pickup at their stores.

Change continues to evolve, and as such technology disrupts market products and service with the birth of new ideas and innovations. Consider the following case study, "Netflix Killed the Video Store":

Netflix, Inc. traded on NASDAQ: NFLX, should be called *"NETFLEX"* as they progressed from physical DVD's and video games delivered and returned via mail which all but ended Blockbuster and other brick and mortar competitors. The company opened on the NASDAQ at $1.21 per share on May 24, 2002 and climbed to an all-time of $391.43 on June 29, trading at $291.57 as of November 8, 2019 it remains impressive in its 17-year history.

Their next progression was to streaming digitally with the advent of SMART TV's, Smart phones and support devices such as ROKU and AppleTV and Chromecast.

Once other competitors found their way to this part of the market such as Amazon Prime, Hulu, Vudu, Redbox and more, they started producing original content through TV shows and movies starring a combination of "A" List movie stars like Sandra Bullock, Keanu Reeves and more as well as emerging young stars putting significant pressure on the customary cord bound TV service that provided these type of originals such as HBO, Showtime and Starz. These previous powerhouses are working to compete by offering their own streaming services; however, are now seen as secondary.

Want to look at planning in progress to evolve with the technology and maintain market share? Look no further than Disney who in a massive power plan pulled all their content rights from the Marvel Cinematic Universe to the tried and true fairy tales from all streaming companies—forging their own platform to compete. They will also offer original content that will only be available through their streaming service delivering a massive blow to competitors while undercutting their pricing.

The marketing concept of Disney is prolific with benefits of long term planning being realized both "vertically" and "horizontally" in their marketing that integrates the brand into all their ventures from Disney World and Disney Land to merchandising, entertainment, travel and tourism and business seminars.

It's Darwinism at its finest—only the strong survive or better those with better plans and flexibility to navigate the changing markets survive, otherwise giants like Sears and JCPenny would continue to rule the consumer department store market.

So how will NETFLIX fair in the next 17 years or longer? According to Martin Tillier, Freelance Writer and Author of "Market Musings" on NASDAQ. com, "Netflix is one resilient company," adding he, "Wouldn't want to bet against them." Tillier concedes "The so-called 'streaming wars' are big news, but one bit of conventional wisdom around the issue is that Disney+, Apple+ and any other plusses that may be coming will be bad for Netflix (NFLX)."[6]

Contingency planning—"what if"—is all about adapting to changing conditions, unexpected outcomes, or changes brought about through technology that from one day to the next render our means and methods obsolete. Vision is only great if it looks long term into the future. That vision propels us forward and keeps us committed to achieving our goals; however, as the landscape changes we need to adjust that vision much like changing our eyeglass prescription as time goes on and our vision changes. At times it may be a simple tweak or minor adjustment, but sometimes it can mean a different pair of glasses completely.

In construction we carry contingency for unforeseen conditions in the form of dollars set aside as a percentage of the total construction cost estimate. In budgets we set up contingencies based on potential scenarios in various accounts to protect against unanticipated expenditures. In business, contingency plans need to be developed based on what risks to that business are prevalent (expected), those we know about, and those we don't see coming (unexpected).

Contingency plans prepare us to deal with unforeseen situations. They can be like Macy's steps to ward off losing market share or being put out of business. In other instances, they can be recovery from major storm damage to plant and equipment.

"Planning is important for every aspect of life. It is crucial for a business because it can be great for preventing risks. In simple words, contingency plans are backup plans that businesses activate only when a disaster or unforeseen situation disrupts the operations of the company or put its employees at risk."[7]

These types of plans are the difference in how quickly we react, how well we react, how much damage or loss we sustain, and whether we survive the crisis. Often, survival of any crisis includes how we are assessed by stakeholders for our handling of the crisis.

In the aftermath of any crisis people focus on the recovery first. Shortly after, and sometimes during, depending on the severity of the loss, people begin to assess our recovery plan. We need to ensure those plans are effective and successful as they can be in a large-scale crisis. Again, without a plan it is difficult to begin marshalling resources or carrying out objectives when no one knows what is expected or what their role is in the exercise. Even more difficult is to try to set up connections and partnerships that often take weeks or months to form and iron out useful and helpful actions for your particular company. This puts undo pressure on an already difficult situation, like if you need to relocate and set up temporary operations to get basic functions running like payroll. At our most challenging and vulnerable times, we as leaders are still expected to keep operations moving.

Whether the crisis be severe market upheavals, budgetary issues, or unlikely weather events, it is not the fact that we are hit with a crisis that calls into question our abilities as leaders. What we would be judged for is our ability or inability to create, have in place, and carry out effective contingency plans to avoid catastrophes.

Chapter Ten

Succession Planning

Ensuring long-term success means we are ready as an organization to carry the vision through until the end, despite the challenges and obstacles we confront along the way. This includes restaffing of important positions through succession planning.

Succession planning is a process for identifying and developing new leaders who can replace existing leaders when they leave or retire. Sometimes, we experience unforeseen long-term absences due to a sudden health crisis or even death. Succession planning increases the availability of experienced and capable employees who are prepared to assume these roles as they become available.[1]

Figure 10.1. Six Steps to Succession Planning

SIX ESSENTIAL STEPS TO SUCCESSION PLANNING

Step 1: Identify Critical Positions

Critical positions within the organization or company that are leadership dependent are the type of positions that go beyond executive levels to include positions that require individuals who can inspire those they lead to accomplish vital tasks within their departments. These are the positions that create gaps in operations, oversight, and management when vacant.

Step 2: Build Success Profiles

Build success profiles that incorporate competencies that ensure success based on the challenges of the position. While positions can be similar with shared functions, responsibilities, or reporting, we need to focus on what attributes are needed in each position for any candidate to be successful. This requires both capability (able) and capacity (ready) in order to handle the degree of rigor associated with the jobs.

- Ability—Aptitude to complete required tasks.
- Technological Know-How—Practical knowledge on how to utilize modern technology in a proficient manner and ability to adapt based on change in needs.
- Behaviors—Attitudes that are positive, effective, and infectious at building and managing teams.
- Strengths—Possessing the ability to perform required tasks consistently and correctly.
- Experiences—Demonstrated mastery of the subject area or operational area to be assigned.

Step 3: Evaluate Staff

Create staff evaluations that are comprehensive and timely and accurately reflect the competencies necessary to demonstrate mastery of the concepts and requirements of the positions.

Nationwide, school districts utilize teacher evaluation models to ensure teachers meet certain performance standards predicated on professional knowledge, instructional planning, instructional delivery, the learning environment, professionalism and communication, and student progress. New Jersey schools, which are rated among the best in the country, use a multitude of teacher evaluation models, including major frameworks recognized nationally and regionally and individual models developed by school districts and approved by the state.

Three of the most common models in use, Danielson, Marshall, and Marzano, all focus on similar elements broken down or grouped within domains. While each has unique differences that focus on certain aspects found to be important to districts, such as community and family outreach within the Marshall model, they also rely on rubrics to gauge performance. These all focus on standards in education and as such measure the teacher's ability to achieve success.

Regardless of the industry you are in, evaluations provide the opportunity to access, inform, guide, support, encourage, and correct behaviors. They are a tool to evaluate and identify superior performers as well as poor performers. It is the superior performers from which we begin to identify successors.

In our world of education, great teachers become candidates for great supervisors, who become candidates for great directors or principals. Likewise, strong principals become candidates for great administrators.

Step 4: Create Professional Development (PD) Programs

Creating PD programs starts with understanding the needs of the organization and then planning PD activities and exercises that enable leaders (current and future) to develop the knowledge and skills they need to address those needs. This includes teaching coping and problem-solving skills to meet various challenges they encounter in the day-to-day or planning activities. A "culture of coaching" means positioning companies to grow and nurture talent.[2] "A coaching culture simply means supporting your employees so that they learn new skills and become greater assets to the company. A management culture that emphasizes training, regular feedback, and opportunities for growth creates a more engaged and energized workforce."[3]

Professional development does this for us, as it provides access and opportunity for all to *learn*, *grow*, and *improve* knowledge and skills that increase effectiveness and target identified areas of need. Yet for some it allows opportunities to showcase their *talent*, *enthusiasm*, and *value add*, which puts them on our radar for advancement—*star search*.

Step 5: Develop Successors

Develop successors who are poised to take on higher roles as those roles become available. Although the plan is to train successor candidates to serve as long-term replacements, we often have opportunities to test them out in short-term situations where critical positions are temporarily available.

Leaves covered under the Family and Medical Leave Act of 1993 (FMLA) requires employers to provide employees with job-protected and unpaid leave for qualified medical and family reasons. This could go up to twelve weeks or three months, which gives us ample opportunity to see how candidates perform at the higher level.

Think about baseball—some players pinch-hit or go in as relievers to close out a troubled inning. In organizations we see these type of relievers as interims, acting supervisors, or temporary employees through a temp service during short stints—like the designated hitter or reliever in baseball. The coach likes nothing better than to have a decent group of pitchers in the bullpen during an important series; however, more important is a healthy farm system or feeder team whose role is to provide experience and training for young players. The understanding is successful players who possess talent and show promise will have the opportunity to move up to the "big show" with a major league team.

Baseball has turned this concept into a business—businesses should model this concept.

Step 6: Build Talent Pools

Building talent pools that are teeming with reliable candidates allows individuals to strive for advancement and prepare themselves for opportunities in the industries they serve. While the danger exists that these candidates can move on to other organizations after we have invested in their progress and prepared them to be successful in leadership roles, we benefit from the goodwill shared over all employees, as they see the possibilities within the organization and industry as a whole. This is motivation in action, as it stimulates interest in moving to the next level, and, more often than not, it creates a culture of trust and investment.

> Talent pools allow organizations to develop employees in areas that align with company competencies and values instead of focusing on developing specific position skills. This allows talent pools to address the biggest challenge with succession planning, which is telling individuals they're part of the plan. Organizations can communicate to a group, "You're the future of the company," instead of telling an individual, "You are our next chief marketing officer."[4]

Succession planning not only demonstrates our commitment to the development of our employees; it also ensures we are working to guard against disruption of key positions within the organization by recognizing and rewarding talent. It takes "cross-training" to the next level to ensure continuity and maintain historical knowledge within our organizations of *how* and *why* things are done or have been done in the past.

History of the organization does not mean we cannot change moving forward; it just means that we have the benefit of knowing why existing systems or decisions are in place. This gives us the necessary understanding of the current situation prior to initiating any new changes and helps us avoid repeating mistakes of the past.

Ever made a change that was unsuccessful because you lacked the benefit of why the practice was in place to begin with, only to have someone come forward after a problem arises and then tell you, that's why we didn't do it this way? Now, you look like you're winging it or simply don't have the right experience.

Succession planning ensures that employees have the right skill set, experience, and knowledge to achieve the strategic goals of the organization within the departments that make it happen. SHRM, the Society for Human Resource Management, recognizes it as, "A focused process for keeping talent in the pipeline."[5] They consider the process to generally take twelve to thirty-six months of preparation, not preselection.[6]

Notice the word *preparation*, not *preselection*. Often, we fall into the pit of preselection when planning for succession, as we assume the assistant can automatically become the chief, lead, or executive. That is not always the case, and we still need to go through the process of looking for the best qualified replacement who possesses the necessary characteristics to assume the higher role—"the right stuff."

I recently had a conversation with an executive director of a major statewide organization who shared this sentiment by stating we are all replaceable; however, the replacement needs to possess the qualities that cannot be taught—they must be inherent. Goes to the adage "the position does not define the person—the person defines the position."

Succession planning simply identifies those in our charge who possess the qualities and qualifications to move ahead within our organizations based on their *talent*, *drive*, and *skill set*. Best of all, they have already been indoctrinated into the culture. These individuals are at the heart of our human resources effort. They are the leaders within the ranks of our organizations who are willing, ready, and able to assume more responsibility and challenge and seek upward mobility. Like talent scouts, it is our responsibility to identify them and then develop them.

MacKay CEO Forums, a Canadian group founded in 2005, consists of 1,000+ members—forward-thinking and action-oriented CEOs, executives, and business owners from across all industries who participate in the highest-impact and least time-intensive professionally led peer learning groups across

Canada. Their mission is to populate the world with inspiring leaders. Great mission—great cause! They recently published a tip sheet on succession planning that includes objectives, principles, definitions, standards, and mastery potential.[7] While there is plenty of information and articles that inform, explain, and support this needed function in succession planning, their tip sheet contains clear, concise, and helpful information in considering the various aspects of succession planning.

While these objectives are similar to other research on the topic, most plans contain three basic elements: *identification, development,* and *retention.* In succession planning the overall objective or specific result we aim to accomplish is to guard against disruption of key positions with available resources.

In basketball, teams employ the *full-court press* to guard against opponents who try to slow the pace and pass inside to a dominant post player. Running a full-court press will force them to play faster and take more undisciplined shots. This allows the team running the press to cover the full length of the court while applying constant pressure on the opponent each time they have the ball. They are guarding against the risk of being scored on. In this example, the players are the "resources," and the coaches decide how to deploy them according to their ability, talent, and skill. With only five on the floor, the bench becomes the critical pool for substitutes.

Coaches need and want talent in the reserve pool or in this case the bench. They work to scout, find, and sign that talent—then develop that talent into starters who win games.

In a sense they are fulfilling the same role for their organization with the ultimate goal of winning that we are tasked with in our own organizations—to accomplish our ultimate goal—the mission. Like them, we need to find players who fit into our system in order to achieve that goal. The better we are at it, the better our results will be each year as we continue to deliver and lead the pack—our competitors.

When it comes to filling or restaffing positions we also want to *pick up the pace* and guard against delays; we too can run a *full-court* PRESS—Professional Retention Expansion Strategies for Successors.

PRESS OBJECTIVES OF SUCCESSION PLANNING

- Advance *Professional* and Leadership Development through programs and opportunities that are inclusive and expected for all individuals and leaders based on position and ability. This means allowing future leaders to get a taste of leadership and grow. This is how we improve current leaders and develop future leaders. Nothing motivates those with potential more than providing opportunity.

- Develop *Retention* Incentives for Identified Successors—This requires an understanding of what each potential successor values and offering a variety or mix of incentives to make them want to stay. Those incentives could be salary, benefits, time off, flexible work schedules, work from home options, or other intrinsic motivations. The key is flexible options that work for both the employee and the company.
- Promote *Expansion* of the Effort to All Executives—This means creating an expectation among your entire executive team through a shared purpose and not just a function of HR. However, the HR department plays a pivotal role in supporting the process with training, maintaining employee information, and technical support for all managers and executives.
- Develop *Strategies* for Creation of Talent Pools—This means organizing successor candidates into "ready-now," "ready soon" within six months, and "ready" within one to three years. This provides managers and executives with a strong pool of possible successors as the time approaches for refilling key position as they become open.

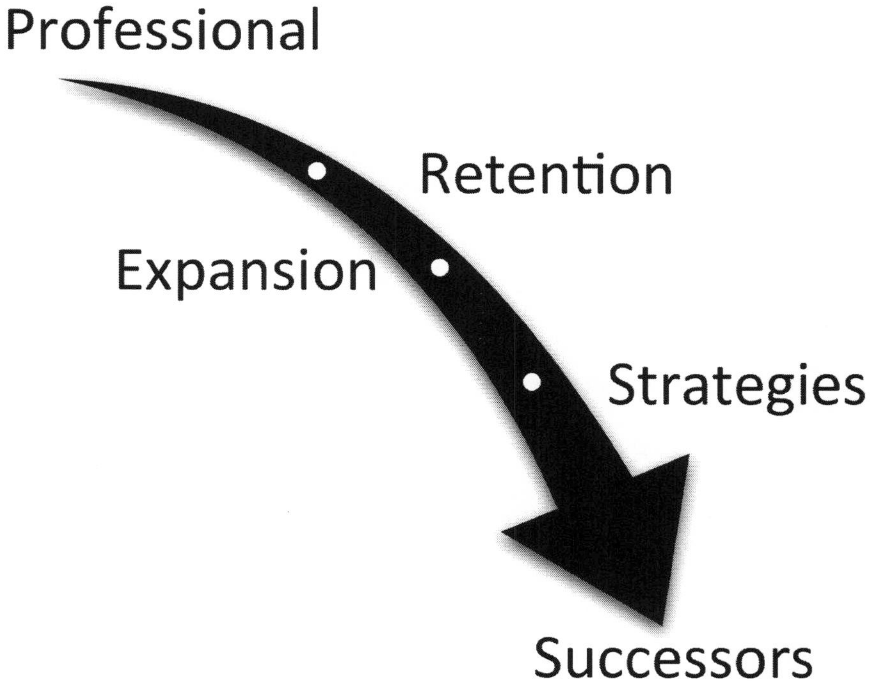

Professional

Retention

Expansion

Strategies

Successors

Figure 10.2. PRESS Objectives for Succession Planning

- Identify *Successors* for Key Positions—This means department managers, supervisors, directors, and executives. These are the positions that manage and direct the organizational drive and initiatives. These individuals ensure we meet our goals and objectives that lead to accomplishment of the mission and attainment of our vision.

When creating and executing succession plans we need to adhere to a set of principles that guide the process and ensure success both from the candidate's perspective and that of the organization. These principles should be predicated on keeping the talent that we have *scouted, identified,* and *signed* from leaving. Paramount among them are these *seven principles for succession planning.*

1. *Create plans that are actionable*—Again, without a plan there is no path to progress; we just see activity. While positions will get filled, it takes longer, especially when you factor in notice provisions, which can be as much as sixty days, depending on the job or industry. Once the plan is in place you need to commit necessary resources to ensure candidates trust the plan.
2. *Forge strong relationships*—Build solid foundations that rely on strength-based attributes for both candidates and development plans. Ensure we are matching the right candidates with the right mentors.
3. *Leave an impression*—Be committed to all aspects of the plan and refuse to settle. This includes scheduling opportunities to build a sense of belonging through connections to individuals and resources within the organization in ways that keep them from becoming isolated or disconnected—the value add of belonging to this company or organization versus going to a "better place."
4. *Be creative*—Make the experience memorable, from the quality of training to the celebrations and activities surrounding your programs, like leadership forums, conferences, and workshop opportunities and retreats. Consider these activities as an investment, not an expense. Both are costs; however, investments produce returns and give off a positive vibe.
5. *Break down silos*—Here, as with all aspects of the operation, we need to think holistically; we need to think *team*. We are all better when we understand the why of what we do, and succession planning is no island. It requires all leaders to assist in the process, as we need to look globally at our resources—this includes human resources.
6. *Determine the need*—Prioritize needs within the organization to ensure available candidates are appropriately placed. This guards against infighting or wasting talent in areas that are less critical or less challenging.

7. *Offer no guarantees*—This is a simple but hard rule to follow for many, as they want to encourage talent to stay and wait for the opening; however, in their panic or worry they overpromise, which creates hard feelings and potential setbacks when the candidate fails to be selected for the vacant position. This can cause a ripple effect among other candidates, and if it happens frequently, it casts doubt about the program's legitimacy.

While succession planning does not guarantee we will always have the right match or the opening at the right time, it does ensure we are meeting our commitment to our workforce and stakeholders by readying today's employees to be tomorrow's leaders. This needs to be an ongoing commitment; however, the true value and benefit of succession planning remains continuity and responsiveness during periods of critical turnover.

Epilogue

Planning requires thought. Its very definition is the act or process of making or carrying out plans, specifically the establishment of goals, policies, and procedures. Successful planning is characterized as *careful*, *deliberate*, and *strategic*.

Throughout this book it has been my goal to underscore one simple point—*proper planning* is at the heart of goal attainment, and it requires attention, understanding, and action. *Strategic planning* allows us to achieve lasting success as our plans go beyond the immediate and encompass our vision to strengthen our brand. When we consider the journey and what is needed to complete that journey, we are putting *strategic planning* into action.

Today's emerging leaders need to consistently realize and master the tools of strategic planning. This requirement will ensure leaders in any organization can create and initiate better plans that reach their goals quicker and more effectively, thus avoiding unnecessary delays or costs associated with poor planning. It starts with understanding the vision and mission of your organization along with having a clear picture of the resources available from within the organization and how to acquire the needed resources from outside the organization in order to combine them into the appropriate blend to fuel the mission. By applying the planning techniques shared in this book you are one step closer to mastering this skill. The 21st century requires us to be quick, flexible, and adaptive as leaders due to the rapid speed of change. We must embrace this fact with a growth mindset to succeed.

While there are a number of planning models to choose from, the Hoshin Planning approach is highly attractive and in step with holistic planning, as it aligns the strategic goals of the organization with the projects and tasks to ensure that efforts are coordinated. This strategic management model is less focused on measures and more on goals and initiatives.[1]

A willingness to apply these principles is what allows us to grow as leaders by putting effective planning into action to acquire our goals and objectives in a way that not only achieves success but also extends the life of that success. This is how we become better leaders in serving our organizations and the people who make them work.

In order to begin that process, we need to know who we are and where we are going—the ultimate destination. This is where vision serves as a guide in determining objectives essential to plot our course in attainment of those goals.

Notes

CHAPTER ONE

1. Morrison, Mike. "The Difference between Goals & Objectives." *RapidBi*. September 9, 2011. Accessed August 18, 2019. https://rapidbi.com/the-difference-between-goals-objectives/.

2. SL Industries, Inc. International Directory of Company Histories, Copyright 2006 Thomson Gale.

3. https://help.rideamigos.com/importance-objectives-goal-setting/.

4. "What Is TDM?" Mobility Lab, February 6, 2019. https://mobilitylab.org/about-us/what-is-tdm/.

5. https://help.rideamigos.com/importance-objectives-goal-setting/.

6. "The Department's FY 2018-19 Priority Performance Goals: U.S. Department of Education." Home. US Department of Education (ED), February 15, 2018. https://www2.ed.gov/about/overview/focus/goals.html.

CHAPTER TWO

1. McCracken, Mareo. "The Real Reason Setting Goals is So Critical to Success: Why Uncovering the Hidden Power of Properly Applied Goals is Something You Need to Do." Inc. November 21, 2107. https://www.inc.com/mareo-mccracken/the-real-reason-setting-goals-is-so-critical-to-success.html.

2. Boss, Jeff. "5 Reasons Why Goal Setting Will Improve Your Focus." *Forbes*. January 19, 2017. Accessed July 30, 2019. https://www.forbes.com/sites/jeffboss/2017/01/19/5-reasons-why-goal-setting-will-improve-your-focus/#54f94ee8534a.

3. Chakraborty, Supriyo, Alun D. Preece, Moustafa Alzantot, Tianwei Xing, Dave Braines, and Mani B. Srivastava. "Deep Learning for Situational Understanding." 2017 20th International Conference on Information Fusion (Fusion) (2017), 1–8.

4. Joseph, Jim. "Why Your Business Needs to Be More Flexible Than Ever." *Entrepreneur.com*. July 4, 2017. Accessed September 15, 2019. https://www.entre preneur.com/article/296735.

5. Ibid.

6. Wright, Tom. "Creating Strategic Focus Areas." *Cascade*. June 5, 2019. Accessed September 13, 2019. https://www.executestrategy.net/blog/strategic-focus-areas.

CHAPTER THREE

1. "Map Reading and Land Navigation," January 2005, Headquarters Department of the Army, accessed September 17, 2019, https://fas.org/irp/doddir/army /fm3-25-26.pdf.

2. Ibid.

3. Robinson, A. H. *Early Thematic Mapping: In the History of Cartography*. Chicago: University of Chicago Press, 1982.

4. *Merriam-Webster*, accessed September 15, 2019, https://www.merriam-webster .com/dictionary/cartography.

5. Wikipedia contributors, "Cartography," *Wikipedia*, accessed September 15, 2019, https://en.wikipedia.org/w/index.php?title=Cartography&oldid=915861335.

6. Dun & Bradstreet Business Directory, accessed September 16, 2019, https:// www.dnb.com/business-directory/company-profiles.rand_mcnally__company.56cb 00f79daef1e0d5e1467db1af1271.html?sitespectflag=TRUE&imok=hoovers&aka _re=1#competitors.

7. Wikipedia contributors, "Rand McNally," *Wikipedia*, accessed September 16, 2019, https://en.wikipedia.org/w/index.php?title=Rand_McNally&oldid=913564518.

8. Bregman, Peter. "How to Discover Your Leadership Blind Spots: Uncovering Your Blind Spots Is Hard. Every Leader Must Ask Themselves These Two Questions." Inc. January 31, 2019. Accessed September 17, 2019.

9. Ibid.

10. Ibid.

11. Map Reading and Land Navigation.

12. "Workflow Diagrams: What They Are, and Where to Use Them." *Kissflow*, September 4, 2019. https://kissflow.com/workflow/workflow-diagrams-jargon-free -guide/.

13. "Work Visually." Lucid. Accessed November 10, 2019. https://www.golucid.co/.

CHAPTER FOUR

1. Michigan University Executive Leadership Program 2019. Accessed August 29, 2019. https://michiganross.umich.edu/programs/executive-education/strategic-leaders-program-vision-strategy-and-managing-organization.

2. National Policy Board for Educational Administration (2015). *Professional Standards for Educational Leaders 2015*. Reston, VA: Author.

3. Son, Hannah. "How to Get Employees Aligned with the Company Vision." *ProSky.com*. January 1, 2018. Accessed September 26, 2019.

4. Ibid.

5. Soldwedel, Perry, and Brett Clark. "Keeping a Strategic Plan Alive." *School Business Affairs* 85, no. 5 (May 2019): 8–11.

6. Ibid.

7. Ibid.

8. Bustin, Greg. "Why Most Company Strategic Plans Fail." *Forbes.com*. September 15, 2014. Accessed September 27, 2019.

9. Ibid.

10. McChesney, Chris, Sean Covey, and Jim Huling. *4 Disciplines of Execution: Getting Strategy Done*. London: Simon & Schuster, 2015.

11. Bustin, Greg. "Why Most Company Strategic Plans Fail." Forbes.com. September 15, 2014. Accessed September 27, 2019.

12. *Bar Rescue*. Directed by Glen GT Taylor and Jay Hunter. Produced by J.D. Roth and Todd A. Nelson for 3 Ball Productions/Eyeworks US. Spike Network 2011, Paramount Network 2018, original air date July 17, 2011.

13. *Hotel Impossible*. Directed by Eli Kabillio. Produced by Rob Green, Bruce David Klein, and Lorri Leighton for Atlas Media Corp. Travel Channel Network, original air date September 4, 2012.

14. *Restaurant Impossible*. Directed by Michael Shea, Hal Grant, Scott Preston, Gordon Recht, Hugh Martin, and Mark Nadeau. Produced by Marc Summers, Justin Wineburgh for Alkemy X and Marc Summers Productions. The Food Network, original air date January 19, 2011.

15. Conway, Byron. "How to Align Employees with Your Company's Mission." Blog: *EmployeeConnect*. Posted February 23, 2018. Accessed September 30, 2019.

CHAPTER FIVE

1. Craig, William. "The Importance of Having a Mission-Driven Company." *Forbes.com*. May 15, 2018. Accessed October 1, 2019.

2. "Master Plan." *Collins English Dictionary*. Accessed October 5, 2019. https://www.collinsdictionary.com/dictionary/english/master-plan.

3. "Alexander Hamilton." George Washington's Mount Vernon. Accessed October 5, 2019. https://www.mountvernon.org/library/digitalhistory/digital-encyclopedia/article/alexander-hamilton/.

4. "10 Essential Facts about Alexander Hamilton on His Birthday." National Constitution Center. Accessed October 5, 2019. https://constitutioncenter.org/blog/10-essential-facts-about-alexander-hamilton/.

5. Sylla, Richard, and David J. Cowen. "Second Report on the Further Provision Necessary for Establishing Public Credit (Report on a National Bank, December 14, 1790): A National Bank Is an Institution of Primary Importance to the Prosperous Administration of the Finances, and Would Be of the Greatest Utility in the Operations Connected with the Support of the Public Credit." In *Alexander Hamilton on Finance, Credit, and Debt*. New York: Columbia University Press, 2018, pp. 117–144.

6. Chernow, Ron. *Alexander Hamilton*. New York, NY: Penguin Group, 2004, p. 372.

7. Ibid., p. 372.

8. "A History of Central Banking in the United States." Federal Reserve Bank of Minneapolis. Accessed October 5, 2019. https://www.minneapolisfed.org/about/more-about-the-fed/history-of-the-fed/history-of-central-banking.

9. "10 Essential Facts about Alexander Hamilton on His Birthday." National Constitution Center—constitutioncenter.org. Accessed October 5, 2019. https://constitutioncenter.org/blog/10-essential-facts-about-alexander-hamilton/.

10. "Alexander Hamilton's Dreams of Industry." It Happened Here in New Jersey. New Jersey Historical Commission. Accessed October 4, 2019. https://nj.gov/state/historical/it-happened-here/ihhnj-er-hamilton.pdf.

11. "Alan Lakein Quotes (*Author of How to Get Control of Your Time and Your Life*)." Goodreads. Accessed October 6, 2019. https://www.goodreads.com/author/quotes/104977.Alan_Lakein.

CHAPTER SIX

1. "Organizational Resources." Strategic Management: Organizational Resources. Accessed October 9, 2019. https://www.introduction-to-management.24xls.com/en105.

2. Wikipedia contributors, "Intangible good," *Wikipedia*, https://en.wikipedia.org/w/index.php?title=Intangible_good&oldid=914072582 (accessed October 9, 2019).

3. "AP Score Scale Table—AP Students—College Board." Accessed October 9, 2019. https://apstudents.collegeboard.org/about-ap-scores/ap-score-scale-table.

4. "Understanding Your Scores—The ACT Test." ACT. Accessed October 9, 2019. https://www.act.org/content/act/en/products-and-services/the-act/scores/understanding-your-scores.html.

5. "Interpreting Your Scores." SAT Suite of Assessments, September 25, 2019. https://collegereadiness.collegeboard.org/sat/scores/understanding-scores/interpreting.

6. *Profiles of American Colleges 2019*. Hauppauge, NY: Barron's Educational Series, Inc., 2018.

7. Ibid.

8. Ibid.

9. Ibid.

10. Ibid.

11. Ibid.

12. "The Best Colleges in America, Ranked." *U.S. News & World Report.* Accessed October 10, 2019. https://www.usnews.com/best-colleges.

13. Publishing, Value Line. "Value Line—The Most Trusted Name in Investment Research." Accessed October 9, 2019. http://www.valueline.com/Stocks/Industries /Industry_Overview__Educational_Services.aspx#.XZ3q00ZKhPY.

14. Ibid.

15. GASBS 34. Accessed October 10, 2019. https://www.gasb.org/jsp/GASB /Document_C/DocumentPage?cid=1176160029121&acceptedDisclaimer=true.

16. New Jersey Administrative Code Title 6A—Department of Education 6A:26-9.1—Capital reserve accounts account § (n.d.); and NJSA 18A Statutes 18A:21-2 —Authorization; establishment of capital reserve account § (n.d.).

17. New Jersey Administrative Code Title 6A—Department of Education 6A:23A-14.4—Establishment of other reserve accounts § (n.d.).

18. NJSA 18A Statutes 18A:7F-38—Limitation upon increase in adjusted tax levy; computations; allowable adjustments § (n.d.).

19. S1701 (SCS/1R) Revises calculation of budget caps and reduces allowable surplus for public school districts. Bills and Joint Resolutions Signed by the Governor.

20. Liberto, Daniel. "Activity-Based Budgeting (ABB) Definition." *Investopedia.* September 20, 2019. https://www.investopedia.com/terms/a/abb.asp.

21. Ibid.

22. Ibid.

23. Ibid.

24. Kagan, Julia. "Zero-Based Budgeting (ZBB)." *Investopedia.* August 27, 2019. https://www.investopedia.com/terms/z/zbb.asp.

25. Ibid.

26. Ibid.

27. "Zero-Based Budgeting: Benefits and Drawbacks." *Investopedia.* April 19, 2019. https://www.investopedia.com/ask/answers/051515/what-are-advantages-and -disadvantages-zerobased-budgeting-accounting.asp.

CHAPTER SEVEN

1. Ong, Cara. "5 Benefits of Strategic Planning." *Envisio.* Accessed October 14, 2019. https://www.envisio.com/blog/benefits-of-strategic-planning.

2. Ramos, Diana. "Construction Cost Estimating: The Basics and Beyond." *Smartsheet.* Accessed October 30, 2019. https://www.smartsheet.com/construction -cost-estimating.

3. "Inflation in Construction 2019—What Should You Carry?" *Construction Analytics*, August 31, 2019. https://edzarenski.com/2018/02/15/inflation-in-construc tion-2019-what-should-you-carry/.

4. "Construction Data." Associated General Contractors of America. Accessed October 16, 2019. https://www.agc.org/learn/construction-data.

5. Merryman, Ray, and US Census Bureau. "US Census Bureau Construction Spending Survey." Census.gov, August 11, 2010. https://www.census.gov/construc tion/c30/c30index.html.

6. Peter Grant, "How Financial Targets Determine Your Strategy," *Global Finance*, 11, no. 3 (1997): 30–34.

7. "Disposition of Property, Plant, and Equipment." *Money*. Accessed October 18, 2019. https://www.money-zine.com/definitions/investing-dictionary/disposition-of -property-plant-and-equipment/.

8. Kramer, Roderick M. "Rethinking Trust." *Harvard Business Review*, August 1, 2014. https://hbr.org/2009/06/rethinking-trust.

9. Covey, Stephen M. R., and Rebecca R. Merrill. *The Speed of Trust: The One Thing That Changes Everything*. Free Press, 2018. https://www.amazon.com /SPEED-Trust-Thing-Changes-Everything/dp/074329730X.

CHAPTER EIGHT

1. "The Value of Debriefing." *Afterburner*, August 14, 2018. https://www.after burner.com/debriefing/.

2. Pepe, Louis J. "Military Leadership Applied to School Business Administra- tion." *School Business Affairs*, April 1, 2019.

3. Ibid.

4. Shikati, Chomwa. "The Price You Will Have to Pay for Your Success." *Medium*. November 28, 2017. https://medium.com/w-i-t/the-price-you-will-have-to -pay-for-your-success-7b0bd97e378f.

5. Movie Quotes Database. Accessed October 20, 2019. http://www.moviequote db.com/movies/wall-street/quote_25564.html.

6. Ibid.

7. Hansbury, Michael. *Something to Be Proud Of*. New Delhi: Epitome Books, 2009. Page 58.

8. "Employee Assistance Programs." Partnership for Workplace Mental Health. Accessed October 26, 2019. http://workplacementalhealth.org/Mental-Health-Topics /Employee-Assistance-Programs.

9. Hymowitz, Kay S. "Is There Anything Grit Can't Do?" *Wall Street Journal*. June 23, 2017. https://www.wsj.com/articles/is-there-anything-grit-cant-do-1498254 238. Accessed October 25, 2019.

10. Brooks, David. "Putting Grit in Its Place." *New York Times*. May 10, 2016. https://www.nytimes.com/2016/05/10/opinion/putting-grit-in-its-place.html. Accessed October 24, 2019.

11. Ibid.

12. Wikipedia contributors, "Inveniam viam," *Wikipedia*, https://en.wikipedia .org/w/index.php?title=Inveniam_viam&oldid=885590135 (accessed October 24, 2019).

13. *True Grit* (1969 film), Wikipedia, https://en.wikipedia.org/w/index .php?title=True_Grit_(1969_film)&oldid=922305189 (accessed October 26, 2019).

14. Ibid.

15. "Investors bank NASDAQ historical prices." Accessed October 24, 2019. https://www.google.com/search?q=Investors+bank+NASDAQ+historical+prices&oq=Investors+bank+NASDAQ+historical+prices&aqs=chrome..69i57.27892j0j7&sourceid=chrome&ie=UTF-8.

16. "Esprit de corps." *Merriam-Webster*. Accessed October 26, 2019. https://www.merriam-webster.com/dictionary/esprit%20de%20corps.

CHAPTER NINE

1. Elliott, Megan. "Amazon Is Completely Destroying These Iconic Stores." *Showbiz Cheat Sheet*, June 12, 2018. https://www.cheatsheet.com/money-career/stores-destroyed-by-amazon.html/.

2. Ibid.

3. Bowman, Jeremy. "Macy's Has a Plan to Fend Off Amazon." *The Motley Fool*. March 24, 2018. https://www.fool.com/investing/2018/03/24/macys-has-a-plan-to-fend-off-amazon.aspx.

4. "Amazon—22 Year Stock Price History." Accessed August 28, 2019. https://www.macrotrends.net/stocks/charts/AMZN/amazon/stock-price-history.

5. "Mail order," *Wikipedia*, https://en.wikipedia.org/w/index.php?title=Mail_order&oldid=916900021 (accessed November 8, 2019).

6. Tillier, Martin. "Netflix (NFLX) Can Survive the Steaming Wars." *NASDAQ*. Accessed November 9, 2019. https://www.nasdaq.com/articles/netflix-nflx-can-survive-the-steaming-wars-2019-11-08.

7. "Contingency Plans: 6 Reasons Why Every Business Should Have Them." *Tweak Your Biz*, April 7, 2019. https://tweakyourbiz.com/global/contingency-plans.

CHAPTER TEN

1. "Succession planning," *Wikipedia*, https://en.wikipedia.org/w/index.php?title=Succession_planning&oldid=909939230 (accessed October 30, 2019).

2. "13 Ways Leaders Can Build A 'Coaching Culture' at Work." *Forbes*. October 7, 2016. https://www.forbes.com/sites/forbescoachescouncil/2016/10/07/13-ways-leaders-can-build-a-coaching-culture-at-work/#30a53aaa44b6.

3. Ibid.

4. Lauby, Sharlyn. "4 Steps for Developing a Talent Pool." *SHRM*. August 16, 2019. https://www.shrm.org/resourcesandtools/hr-topics/talent-acquisition/pages/4-steps-for-developing-a-talent-pool.aspx.

5. "The Voice of All Things Work." *SHRM*, October 30, 2019. https://www.shrm.org/pages/default.aspx.

6. Ibid.

7. "Succession Planning Objectives, Principles, and Definitions." MacKay CEO Forums. Accessed October 31, 2019. https://mackayceoforums.com/tipsheets/succession-planning-objectives-principles-definitions/.

EPILOGUE

1. Smith, Rachel, and Joe Smith. "16 Strategic Planning Models To Consider." *ClearPoint Strategy*, August 6, 2019. https://www.clearpointstrategy.com/strategic-planning-models/.

References

Boss, Jeff. "5 Reasons Why Goal Setting Will Improve Your Focus." *Forbes*. January 19, 2017. Accessed July 30, 2019. https://www.forbes.com/sites/jeffboss/2017/01/19/5 -reasons-why-goal-setting-will-improve-your-focus/#54f94ee8534a.

Bowman, Jeremy. "Macy's Has a Plan to Fend Off Amazon." *The Motley Fool*. March 24, 2018. https://www.fool.com/investing/2018/03/24/macys-has-a-plan -to-fend-off-amazon.aspx.

Bregman, Peter. "How to Discover Your Leadership Blind Spots: Uncovering Your Blind Spots Is Hard. Every Leader Must Ask Themselves These Two Questions." *Inc*. January 31, 2019. Accessed September 17, 2019.

Brooks, David. "Putting Grit in Its Place." *New York Times*. May 10, 2016. https:// www.nytimes.com/2016/05/10/opinion/putting-grit-in-its-place.html. Accessed October 24, 2019.

Bustin, Greg. "Why Most Company Strategic Plans Fail." *Forbes*. September 15, 2014. Accessed September 27, 2019.

Conway, Byron. "How to Align Employees with Your Company's Mission." Blog: *EmployeeConnect*. Posted February 23, 2018. Accessed September 30, 2019.

Covey, Stephen M. R., and Rebecca R. Merrill. *The Speed of Trust: The One Thing That Changes Everything*. Free Press, 2018. https://www.amazon.com/SPEED -Trust-Thing-Changes-Everything/dp/074329730X.

Chakraborty, Supriyo, Alun D. Preece, Moustafa Alzantot, Tianwei Xing, Dave Braines, and Mani B. Srivastava. "Deep Learning for Situational Understanding." 2017 20th International Conference on Information Fusion (Fusion) (2017), 1–8.

Chernow, Ron. *Alexander Hamilton*. New York, NY: Penguin Group, 2004.

Craig, William. "The Importance of Having a Mission-Driven Company." *Forbes*. May 15, 2018. Accessed October 1, 2019.

Elliott, Megan. "Amazon Is Completely Destroying These Iconic Stores." *Showbiz Cheat Sheet*, June 12, 2018. https://www.cheatsheet.com/money-career/stores -destroyed-by-amazon.html/.

Grant, Peter. "How Financial Targets Determine Your Strategy," *Global Finance* 11, no. 3 (1997): 30–34.

Hansbury, Michael. *Something to Be Proud Of.* New Delhi: Epitome Books, 2009.

Hymowitz, Kay S. "Is There Anything Grit Can't Do?" *Wall Street Journal.* June 23, 2017. https://www.wsj.com/articles/is-there-anything-grit-cant-do-1498254238. Accessed October 25, 2019.

Joseph, Jim. "Why Your Business Needs to Be More Flexible than Ever." *Entrepreneur.com.* July 4, 2017. Accessed September 15, 2019. https://www.entrepreneur.com/article/296735.

Kagan, Julia. "Zero-Based Budgeting (ZBB)." *Investopedia.* August 27, 2019. https://www.investopedia.com/terms/z/zbb.asp.

Kramer, Roderick M. "Rethinking Trust." *Harvard Business Review.* August 1, 2014. https://hbr.org/2009/06/rethinking-trust.

Lauby, Sharlyn. "4 Steps for Developing a Talent Pool." *SHRM.* August 16, 2019. https://www.shrm.org/resourcesandtools/hr-topics/talent-acquisition/pages/4-steps-for-developing-a-talent-pool.aspx.

Liberto, Daniel. "Activity-Based Budgeting (ABB) Definition." *Investopedia.* September 20, 2019. https://www.investopedia.com/terms/a/abb.asp.

Merryman, Ray, and US Census Bureau. "US Census Bureau Construction Spending Survey." Census.gov, August 11, 2010. https://www.census.gov/construction/c30/c30index.html.

McChesney, Chris, Sean Covey, and Jim Huling. *4 Disciplines of Execution: Getting Strategy Done.* London: Simon & Schuster, 2015.

McCracken, Mareo. "The Real Reason Setting Goals Is So Critical to Success: Why Uncovering the Hidden Power of Properly Applied Goals Is Something You Need to Do." *Inc.* November 21, 2107. https://www.inc.com/mareo-mccracken/the-real-reason-setting-goals-is-so-critical-to-success.html.

Morrison, Mike. "The Difference between Goals and Objectives." *RapidBi.* September 9, 2011. Accessed August 18, 2019. https://rapidbi.com/the-difference-between-goals-objectives/.

Ong, Cara. "5 Benefits of Strategic Planning." *Envisio.* Accessed October 14, 2019. https://www.envisio.com/blog/benefits-of-strategic-planning.

Pepe, Louis J. "Military Leadership Applied to School Business Administration." *School Business Affairs*, April 1, 2019.

Ramos, Diana. "Construction Cost Estimating: The Basics and Beyond." *Smartsheet.* Accessed October 30, 2019. https://www.smartsheet.com/construction-cost-estimating.

Robinson, A. H. *Early Thematic Mapping: In the History of Cartography.* Chicago: University of Chicago Press, 1982.

Shikati, Chomwa. "The Price You Will Have to Pay for Your Success." *Medium.* November 28, 2017. https://medium.com/w-i-t/the-price-you-will-have-to-pay-for-your-success-7b0bd97e378f.

Soldwedel, Perry, and Brett Clark. "Keeping a Strategic Plan Alive." *School Business Affairs* 85, no. 5 (May 2019): 8–11.

Son, Hannah. "How to get Employees Aligned with the Company Vision." *ProSky .com*. January 1, 2018. Accessed September 26, 2019.

Sylla, Richard, and David J. Cowen. "Second Report on the Further Provision Necessary for Establishing Public Credit (Report on a National Bank, December 14, 1790): A National Bank Is an Institution of Primary Importance to the Prosperous Administration of the Finances, and Would Be of the Greatest Utility in the Operations Connected with the Support of the Public Credit." In *Alexander Hamilton on Finance, Credit, and Debt*, 117–44. New York: Columbia University Press, 2018.

Tillier, Martin. "Netflix (NFLX) Can Survive the Steaming Wars." *NASDAQ*. Accessed November 9, 2019. https://www.nasdaq.com/articles/netflix-nflx-can -survive-the-steaming-wars-2019-11-08.

Wright, Tom. "Creating Strategic Focus Areas." *Cascade*. June 5, 2019. Accessed September 13, 2019. https://www.executestrategy.net/blog/strategic-focus-areas.

About the Author

Louis J. Pepe is the author of *Smarter Decision Making: Avoiding Poor Decisions Effective Listening*, the first in the RBL series on leadership.

He is the assistant superintendent/CFO for the City of Summit Public Schools in Union County, New Jersey. He has more than thirty years of leadership experience between military and private and public service focused on leadership, management, operations, and administration.

Lou is a speaker, mentor, and adjunct professor at Montclair State University. His knowledge and success has positioned him as a go-to resource for other professionals throughout the industry. A member of the Oxford Roundtable, Lou presented on issues in financing public education in America at Oxford University in Oxford England in 2005.

He is the president and owner of Lou Pepe Presentations, LLC, consulting on effective management strategies and leadership training through presentations designed for workshops, seminars, conferences, and business meetings.

As a keynote speaker and presenter, Lou has engaged audiences across the country with his down-to-earth, practical advice and insights into today's challenges in managing people and situations to accomplish organizational goals and objectives.

His blog site, http://businessedissues.blogspot.com/, has gained readership from countries all over the world and was featured as "best of blogs" by the American Association of School Administrators.

HONORS AND AWARDS

- School Business Administrator of the Year—New Jersey Association of School Business Officials 2018

- Distinguished Service Award—New Jersey Association of School Business Officials 2018
- Eagle Award 2015 ASBO—Association of School Business Officials International Leadership Achievement Awards
- Pinnacle of Achievement for Innovative Ideas in the Field of School Business 2007 ASBO—Association of School Business Officials International
- Oxford Roundtable 2005—Speaker on Issues in Financing Public Education in America, Oxford University, Oxford England.
- Recipient of the US Army Commendation Medal (ARCOM) oak leaf cluster and Achievement Medal

EDUCATION

Mr. Pepe earned his bachelor's degree in international business and business administration from Ramapo College of New Jersey and an MBA in finance from William Paterson University's Christos M. Cotsakos College of Business.

BACKGROUND

Prior to entering the field of education, Mr. Pepe was a scanning administrator for the Atlantic & Pacific Tea Company and administrative assistant for SL Industries and served in the US Army Signal Corps as a tactical signal operator 72E, in Darmstadt Germany, USAISC as MARS Radio operator at Fort Campbell Kentucky, and as an Automated Telecommunications Specialist 72G Shift Supervisor with the 66th Military Intelligence Brigade, Munich Germany. Through these experiences, Mr. Pepe developed leadership skills in team building, management, and communications.

He is currently a past president of New Jersey Association of School Business Officials, has served two terms as a councilman at large in his home community, and continues to serve as a mentor for New Jersey Department of Education State Certification Program. Lou is on faculty at Montclair State University as an adjunct professor in the graduate program in education.

He and his wife live in Lincoln Park, New Jersey, and have two daughters and two grandchildren.